# Awaiting Christmas

## A Family Devotional for Advent

TJ Torgerson

Chuck Sanford

# DEDICATIONS

T.J. - To my wonderful wife, Nacomi and my three sons;
Caleb, Zack, and Joe.

Chuck – To my loving wife, Kayte. A new family tradition.

The ornaments for your Jesse Tree can found at
www.GoodhopeNaz.com/jessetree

# TABLE OF CONTENTS

# CONTENTS CONTINUED

# ACKNOWLEDGMENTS

I would like to thank the wonderful people at Goodhope Church of the Nazarene; a pastor couldn't ask for a better group of people. Thank you to Robert Minkler, Brenda Kelley, Kayte Sanford, and Ellen Dunn for their contributions in getting this book done. Lastly, a special thanks to Chuck Sanford who stepped in to make sure this book was finished on time.

– From T.J

I would like to thank my mom and dad, who raised me to know the value of a good story. My wife for always reminding me of the best story. My church for giving me a place to tell the story. Finally, my son Isaac, for always listening to you dad's stories.

– From Chuck

# INTRODUCTION

## WHAT IS ADVENT?

Advent begins four Sundays before Christmas. It can begin on any date between November 27th and December 3rd. The last day of Advent is always on Christmas Eve. The Christmas season begins on Christmas Day and lasts until Epiphany on January 6th. Because of the changing start date of Advent, the Advent season can last anywhere between 22 and 28 days.

The word "Advent" stems from the Latin word *adventus* which means, "coming." Advent is a wonderful time to anticipate the coming of Christ into the world. Part of the observance of Advent is to consider how God's people, the nation of Israel, patiently waited for the coming of the promised Messiah. Today, Advent reminds us that we too patiently and expectantly wait for the triumphal return of Christ.

It seems that in today's culture of immediate gratification, we begin the *Christmas frenzy* before we finish eating our Thanksgiving leftovers. Perhaps this wouldn't be so bad if this frenzy had a hint of Christ. Instead, we run from sale to sale, focused on everything except Christ.

There is a war on Christmas. I do not mean where Christian folks get filled with contempt when the minimum wage worker at the local chain store doesn't say, "Merry Christmas" to them as they max out their credit cards buying things no one needs or wants. Rather, I mean that in our frenzy we forget the heart and spirit of Christ. The real threat to Christmas is that it's being taken over by greed and materialism.

We get swallowed up by consumerism, and then we get weighed down by guilt and despair when we realize we cannot afford the things everyone says we need to buy. It is in this materialistic frenzy that we begin to believe that our savior is our bank account. Our *hope, love, joy,* and *peace* become based on how much we can buy and how much we receive. Our wallets either put us in a place of pride about our wealth, or a place of despair because we simply cannot keep up with the Joneses. Christ is not found in any of that.

We challenge you this season to avoid the *Christmas frenzy*. Instead, focus on Advent. Focus on the need we have for the kind of saving that Christ does. Anticipate Jesus the same way the Ancient Israelites anticipated the coming of the promised Messiah. Instead of rushing through the season, let's wait for Him, seek Him, and hope for Him. Allow the heart and mind of Christ to envelope us. That is what observing Advent is all about!

## WHAT IS A JESSE TREE?

In Isaiah chapter 11, there is a prophecy concerning the coming of Jesus into the world. This prophecy was uttered 700 years before the birth of Christ by the Prophet Isaiah:

> *A shoot will come up from the stump of Jesse;*
> *from his roots a Branch will bear fruit.*
> *The Spirit of the* Lord *will rest on him—*
> *the Spirit of wisdom and of understanding,*
> *the Spirit of counsel and of might,*
> *the Spirit of the knowledge and fear of the* Lord *—*
> *and he will delight in the fear of the* Lord. *(NIV)*

This prophecy points to the lineage of Jesse (the father of King David) and says the promised Messiah will come from that family. Christians over the ages have celebrated the tradition of the Jesse Tree. This tradition looks at the history of God's activity in the world as recorded in Scripture. The Jesse Tree shows how with each generation, Israel moved that much closer to the promised Christ who would save His people.

The tradition of the Jesse Tree began in medieval times and was a visual way to tell the story of the Bible from Creation to Jesus. Early depictions of the "Jesse

Tree" were wooden carvings or stained glass. Over time, the imagery morphed into an Advent/Christmas tradition and is now used by many families and churches during the Advent season to remember how God has worked in human history.

During each day of Advent, a story is told from Scripture and an accompanying ornament is hung on the Jesse Tree. Each time the family gathers around the tree for the next story, the ornaments are then used as visual reminders of the journey the family has gone through during Advent. The ornaments and stories are reminders to us of God's faithfulness to humanity throughout history.

The ornaments for your Jesse Tree can found at
www.GoodhopeNaz.com/jessetree

## THE COLORS OF ADVENT[1]

Over the centuries, the Christian Church has adopted certain colors to be used at different times during the church year. Different groups of Christians use slightly different colors, but most of us use the following colors for the Advent and Christmas season.

Purple – This is the color of royalty. It is used to signify and welcome the coming king. It also signifies preparation, pain, suffering, and penance. It should bring to mind the coming birth of Christ, as well as foreshadow His death. It is used the first, second, and fourth weeks of Advent.

Pink – This color represents joy and happiness. While Advent is a time of reflection and preparation, it is good to be reminded that there is joy to be found in our anticipation of Christmas. Pink is used on the third Sunday of Advent, although some traditions reserve pink for the fourth Sunday.

Gold – Gold symbolizes that which is precious and valuable. It reminds us of majesty, joy, and celebration, and is a symbol of the presence of God. Yellow can be used as a substitute for gold. Yellow symbolizes light, renewal and hope. Yellow should remind us of the light that has come into the world. Gold/Yellow is used after Advent season and during the Christmas season (Dec 25th – Jan 6th).

White (used alongside gold/yellow) – White symbolizes purity, virtue, respect, reverence, and holiness. White is used after Advent and during the Christmas season (December 25th – January 6th).

## HOW TO USE THIS BOOK

This book is a devotional resource for individual or family use. It is designed to assist you and your family, to worship together, during the Advent season. There are three components involved in this devotional. First. there is the Advent readings and candle lighting. Next is the Bible story reading and reflection. Last is the Jesse Tree ornament.

### EACH YEAR

This book is designed so that it can be used each year and, we hope, develop into a family tradition. Because Advent can last anywhere between 22 and 28 days, some years all the stories will be read, while other years some stories will need to be skipped. At the beginning of Advent season, refer to the chart on page 7. This chart will tell you the date Advent begins and what day Christmas is on.

Begin your devotional time on the appropriate date (always a Sunday) with the candle lighting (pages 8-17) and the Creation story (page 20).  The following day, continue to the next story. Skip the story if Christmas Day for that year is grayed out. For example: if Christmas is on a Monday this year, you would skip the story about Tamar on page 34 because the "M" at the top of the page is grayed out (M). Instead, move to the following story about Joseph on page 36.

### EACH DAY

Your devotional time each day starts with the Advent candle reading. We have provided five different readings: one for each of the four weeks of Advent, and one for Christmas. The readings are found on the following pages: Hope, page 8; Love, page 10; Joy, page 12; Peace, page 14; and Christ, page 16. These are short responsive readings for the family that can also be used for personal reflection.

During the responsive reading time, there is a candle lighting service. Light the candle as instructed in the reading. Children can take turns lighting the candle each evening, and of course, always have adult supervision around open flames. After the candle lighting ceremony is the story time. Begin story time by using the ornaments to review the stories that have already been read.

After you have reviewed the ornaments that have already been hung, show the new ornament and have a family member hang it. While the candle is burning, read the current day's story. After the story is read, take some time and discuss it with your family or reflect on it as an individual. After an appropriate amount of discussion and reflection, pray together and read the benediction over your family. The benedictions are found on the following pages: Hope, page 9; Love, page 11; Joy, page 13; Peace, page 15; and Christ, page 17. After the benediction is read, select a family member to extinguish the candle, and say together, "Come Lord Jesus."

**NOTE:** The Bible tells things as they happened in history. As a result, some Bible stories are not G-rated. We have taken efforts to be both true to the story and present it in a family-friendly manner. However, it is recommended that a parent or guardian read through the stories beforehand, because the parent or guardian, not the authors of this book, should make the decision of what stories your family hears and how they hear them.

YOU WILL NEED

- **This book**
- **5 Candles**
  - ○ The candles can be any shape, size, or color. If you would like to have a traditional Advent wreath, you will need 1 white candle (the Christ candle), 3 purple candles (weeks 1, 2, 4) and a pink candle (week 3).
- **A Jesse Tree**
  - ○ You will need something to use as your Jesse Tree. Use your imagination and creativity. It is recommended that it is something separate than your Christmas Tree. The Jesse Tree simply needs to be something on which you can hang your ornaments. There are a lot of great ideas on Pinterest.[2]
- **Jesse Tree Ornaments**
  - ○ The Jesse Tree Ornaments can be downloaded and printed from *www.GoodhopeNaz.com/jessetree* free of charge. Take the time to carefully cut them out. If possible laminate the ornaments so they hold up to repeated use over the years. Alternatively, you can create your own ornaments to represent each story.
- **Christmas Ornament Hooks**
  - ○ Can be purchased at any local retailer. Use a hole punch to make a hole in the ornament insert the hook to hang the ornament on your Jesse Tree.
- **Two Bookmarks**
  - ○ Each day during this devotional you will be looking at a couple different pages. It is recommended you place a bookmark at the Advent candle reading page for the week, as well as one to mark which story you are on.
- **10- 15 minutes each day**
  - ○ We understand how busy this time of year can be. We have kept each devotional short; about 10-15 minutes each day. Think of this time as an investment. You may be amazed at how this investment will help you keep focused on what matters during this season.

## ADVENT CHART

| Year | Begins | Christmas | Year | Begins | Christmas |
|------|--------|-----------|------|--------|-----------|
| 2017 | Dec 3 | M | 2034 | Dec 3 | M |
| 2018 | Dec 2 | TU | 2035 | Dec 2 | T |
| 2019 | Dec 1 | W | 2036 | Nov 30 | TH |
| 2020 | Nov 29 | F | 2037 | Nov 29 | F |
| 2021 | Nov 28 | SA | 2038 | Nov 28 | SA |
| 2022 | Nov 27 | SU | 2039 | Nov 27 | SU |
| 2023 | Dec 3 | M | 2040 | Dec 2 | T |
| 2024 | Dec 1 | W | 2041 | Dec 1 | W |
| 2025 | Nov 30 | TH | 2042 | Nov 30 | TH |
| 2026 | Nov 29 | F | 2043 | Nov 29 | F |
| 2027 | Nov 28 | SA | 2044 | Nov 27 | SU |
| 2028 | Dec 3 | M | 2045 | Dec 3 | M |
| 2029 | Dec 2 | T | 2046 | Dec 2 | T |
| 2030 | Dec 1 | W | 2047 | Dec 1 | W |
| 2031 | Nov 30 | TH | 2048 | Nov 29 | TH |
| 2032 | Nov 28 | SA | 2049 | Nov 28 | SA |
| 2033 | Nov 27 | SU | 2050 | Nov 27 | SU |

# HOPE CANDLE

## THE FIRST WEEK OF ADVENT

SU M TU W TH F SA

**Responsive Reading**

> **Reader:** I lift up my eyes to the hills — where does my help come from?
>
> **All:** My help comes from the Lord, the Maker of heaven and earth.[3]
>
> **Reader:** Why are we lighting the candle of hope?
>
> **Adult:** Advent is a time to wait with hope. The world needs a savior. Long ago, God promised that He would send someone to save people from their sins. On the very first Christmas, God kept His promise. We now wait and prepare our hearts to celebrate Christmas.

**Candle Lighting**

> Light the first purple candle, saying: *We light the candle of hope to remind us that Jesus is the hope of the world!*

**Ornament**

> Before each story, point to the ornaments already hung and review the stories that each represents. After all of the stories have been reviewed, show the new ornament and have someone hang it. After the story, talk about how the picture and the story are related.

**Story**

Read the story for the day and use the discussion points at the end of each story.

**Pray**

Take some time to pray with each other as a family. Focus your prayers on the theme of hope and on the lesson learned from each story.

**Benediction**[4]

It would be appropriate for parents to pray the blessing found below over their children. If doing the book as a couple, the couple may pray the blessing over each other. If you find yourself alone during this Advent season, I humbly speak the blessing over you

*May the God of hope fill you with all joy and peace as you trust in him, so that you may overflow with hope by the power of the Holy Spirit. - Romans 15:13 (NIV)*

**Finish**

Extinguish the Candle Saying: *"Come Lord Jesus"* (Rev 22:20)

The ornaments for your Jesse Tree can be found at
www.GoodhopeNaz.com/jessetree

# LOVE CANDLE

## THE SECOND WEEK OF ADVENT

SU M TU W TH F SA

**Responsive Reading:**

> **Reader**: I lift up my eyes to the hills — where does my help come from?

> **All**: My help comes from the LORD, the Maker of heaven and earth. [3]

> **Reader**: Why are we lighting a candle of love?

> **Adult**: Advent is a time to prepare our hearts. This week, we remember God's unconditional love for us. We remember that it is our privilege to share this love with those around us. We wait together for Christmas, when God's love took on flesh.

**Candle Lighting:**

> Light two purple candles saying: *We light the candle of love to remember that we love because He first loved us*

**Ornament:**

> Before each story, point to the ornaments already hung and review the stories that each represent. After each of the stories are reviewed, show the new ornament and have someone hang it. After the story, talk about how the picture and the story are related.

**Story**

Read the story for the day and use the discussion points at the end of each story.

**Pray**

Take some time to pray with each other as a family. Focus your prayers on the theme of love and on the lesson learned from each story.

**Benediction**

It would be appropriate for parents to pray the blessing found below over their children. If doing the book as a couple, the couple may pray the blessing over each other. If you find yourself alone during this Advent season, I humbly speak the blessing over you.

*May our Lord Jesus Christ himself and God our Father, who loved us and by his grace gave us eternal encouragement and good hope, encourage your hearts and strengthen you in every good deed and word. Through Jesus Christ our Lord Amen.*
*−2 Thessalonians 2:16-17 (NIV)*

**Finish**

Extinguish the Candle Saying: *"Come Lord Jesus"* (Rev 22:20)

# JOY CANDLE

THE THIRD WEEK OF ADVENT

SU M TU W TH F SA

**Responsive Reading:**

> **Reader:** I lift up my eyes to the hills— where does my help come from?

> **All:** My help comes from the LORD, the Maker of heaven and earth. ³

> **Reader:** Why are we lighting the candle of joy?

> **Adult:** Advent is a time to prepare our hearts. This week we remember the joy Jesus brings. Even though we can't see Him, we love Him. And we are filled with an inexpressible and glorious joy.

**Candle Lighting:**

> Light two purple and a pink candle saying: *We light the candle of joy to remember the joy Christ brings.*

**Ornament:**

> Before each story point to the ornaments already hung and review the stories that each represents. After each of the stories are reviewed show the new ornament and have someone hang it. After the story talk about how the picture and the story are related.

**Story**

Read the story for the day and use the discussion points at the end of each story.

**Pray**

Take some time to pray with each other as a family. Focus your prayers on the theme of joy and on the lesson learned from each story.

**Benediction**

It would be appropriate for parents to pray the blessing found below over their children. If doing the book as a couple, the couple may pray the blessing over each other. If you find yourself alone during this Advent season, I humbly speak the blessing over you.

*To him who is able to keep you from stumbling and to present you before his glorious presence without fault and with great joy— to the only God our Savior be glory, majesty, power and authority, through Jesus Christ our Lord, before all ages, now and forevermore! Amen.*
*–Jude 1:24-25 (NIV)*

**Finish**

Extinguish the Candle Saying: *"Come Lord Jesus"* (Rev 22:20)

# PEACE CANDLE

## THE FOURTH WEEK OF ADVENT

SU M TU W TH F SA

**Responsive Reading:**

**Reader**: I lift up my eyes to the hills— where does my help come from?

**All:** My help comes from the LORD, the Maker of heaven and earth.[3]

**Reader:** Why are we lighting the candle of peace?

**Adult:** Advent is a time to prepare our hearts. This week we remember the peace He brings and wait for the Prince of Peace.

**Candle Lighting:**

Light three purple and a pink candle saying: *We light the candle of peace as we wait for the Prince of Peace.*

**Ornament:**

Before each story point to the ornaments already hung and review the stories that each represents. After each of the stories are reviewed show the new ornament and have someone hang it. After the story talk about how the picture and the story are related.

**Story**

Read the story for the day and use the discussion points at the end of each story.

**Pray**

Take some time to pray with each other as a family. Focus your prayers on the theme of peace and on the lesson learned from the story.

**Benediction**

It would be appropriate for parents to pray the blessing found below over their children. If doing the book as a couple, the couple may pray the blessing over each other. If you find yourself alone during this Advent season, I humbly speak the blessing over you.

*[May] you experience God's peace, which is far more wonderful than the human mind can understand. His peace will keep your thoughts and your hearts quiet and at rest as you trust in Christ Jesus.*
–Philippians 4:7 (TLB)

**Finish**

Extinguish the Candle Saying: *"Come Lord Jesus"* (Rev 22:20)

# CHRIST CANDLE

CHRISTMAS DAY

SU M TU W TH F SA

**Responsive Reading:**
> **Reader**: I lift up my eyes to the hills— where does my help come from?
>
> **All:** My help comes from the LORD, the Maker of heaven and earth.[3]
>
> **Reader:** Why are we lighting the Christ candle?
>
> **Adult:** We light the Christ candle because Christ our light came into the world on Christmas day. We are the keepers of His light until he comes again.

**Candle Lighting:**
> Light all the candles saying: *Our hope is found in Him. All love flows from Him. He is our joy and our peace. Jesus the light of the world has come.*

**Ornament:**
> Before each story point to the ornaments already hung and review the stories that each represents. After each of the stories are reviewed show the new ornament and have someone hang it. After the story talk about how the picture and the story are related.

**Story**

> Read the story for the day and use the discussion points at the end of each story.

**Pray**

> Take some time to pray with each other as a family. Focus your prayers on the themes of hope, love, joy, and peace and on the lesson learned from the story.

**Benediction**

> It would be appropriate for parents to pray the blessing found below over their children. If doing the book as a couple, the couple may pray the blessing over each other. If you find yourself alone during this Advent season, I humbly speak the blessing over you.

*Grace and peace to you from "he who is," and who was, and who is still to come, … and from Jesus Christ — the faithful witness, the firstborn from among the dead, the ruler over the kings of the earth*
– Revelation 1:4-5 (NET)

**Finish**

> Extinguish the Candle Saying: *"Come Lord Jesus"* (Rev 22:20)

# CREATION

SU M TU W TH F SA

*First this: God created the Heavens and Earth—all you see, all you don't see. Earth was a soup of nothingness, a bottomless emptiness, an inky blackness. God's Spirit brooded like a bird above the watery abyss. God spoke: "Light!" And light appeared. God saw that light was good and separated light from dark. – Genesis 1:1-4 (MSG)*

Before there was me and before there was you; before there were trees and before there were bees; before your mom and dad were born and long before your hound dog, Charlie, could howl at the moon; before there was dirt and before there was mud; before there were whales and before there were birds; there was God and nothing else.

Then God created. He made everything that we can see and everything we cannot see. God made everything out of nothing at all! The Bible teaches us that before God first brought "stuff" into existence, it was dark, empty, and chaotic. So God, with great love, spoke into the darkness declaring -- "Light!" -- and before the echo of His words faded, the universe was filled with light.

Then God began to bring order to the chaos. He separated the darkness from the light; He separated night from day; He separated the dirt from the water and the water from the sky; and when everything was just where it should be, God smiled and said, "It is good."

But God's Creation was still empty. So God made plants to fill the land and flowers to paint the fields. He planted trees whose roots would reach deep into the dirt and whose branches would stretch out to the sky. God gave the plants the ability to produce seeds so that the land would continually be filled. In the sky, He hung the stars and the Moon and the Sun, each in its special place. The stars hung in the night sky and the Sun lit up the day. When God looked at all the plants and at the Sun, Moon, and stars, He smiled and said, "It is good."

But God was not finished. The land, sea, and sky were filled, but God had more in mind, so He poured more life into them! In the seas he placed fish, crabs, whales, sharks, dolphins, octopi, and turtles --- just to name a few. In the sky he placed the vulture, the eagle, the sparrow, the hummingbird, the crow, the pelican and the stork --- just to name a few. On the land he placed the horse, the cow, the lion, the cheetah, the elephant, the giraffe, the chimpanzee, and the hound dog --- just to name a few. Now God's creation was overflowing with life. God smiled and said, "This is good!"

But God still was not finished. He needed to add the final touch. Just as with any great artist, He needed to place His signature on His work. Just like any great king, the work needed His stamp of approval. So God created the human. The human was created in God's image; both male and female were created in the image of God. God gave the man and the woman dominion over the creation and gave them food to eat and life to enjoy. God looked at all of His work and determined that it was finished. God, with great joy, said, "It is good -- it is VERY GOOD!" Then God rested.

And they all lived happily ever after…. or did they?

*Take some time today to enjoy God's creation. Share with your family what part of Creation you enjoy most.*

# ADAM AND EVE

SU M TU W TH F SA

*Cursed is the ground because of you... – Gen. 3:17b (NIV)*

What happened? Not long ago, God was smiling and His creation was VERY GOOD! But not anymore. Now God looked Adam in the eye and, speaking as clearly as He spoke when He spoke light into existence, said, "Because of you creation is cursed. You cannot live in the garden anymore."

Everything changed so fast. The Bible doesn't say this, but I think that Adam, Eve, and God lingered for a moment in Eden, crying together over what was lost. What caused this rift between Adam, Eve, and the Creator? Who was to blame?

In the garden, among all the other trees, God planted two special trees: the Tree of Life and the Forbidden Tree. Adam was allowed to eat from any of the trees. He could have bananas for breakfast, lemons for lunch, and dates for dinner. He could eat mangos, melons, and macadamia nuts. He could have okra, onions, oranges, apples, artichokes and zucchini! Adam and Eve could eat anything they wanted. They could even eat from the Tree of Life and live forever.

They could eat anything, that is, except for fruit from the Forbidden Tree. God commanded them – God warned them – God clearly told them, "Do not eat from this tree or you will die!" That seems strange doesn't it? Why would God plant a tree in the garden that could turn something from "very good" into a deadly curse? Ah ha! You may be thinking – "It was God's fault! God caused the rift!" No. It was not God's fault.

A crafty, sneaky serpent slithered its way into the garden. The serpent saw how much God loved Adam and Eve, how much Adam and Eve loved one another, and how much Adam and Eve loved God. This made that crafty old snake jealous. The snake hated that God was getting all the attention! It hated the special relationship they had. So the snake slithered its way into the picture, looking to get some attention of its own, looking to disrupt this relationship.

The sly snake crafted a plan. It fabricated some lies and said with its forked tongue, "Hey Eve, hey Adam. You need to try some of this fruit. Trust me when I tell you it is delicious! I mean how can something so beautiful be bad for you?"

Eve and Adam began to wonder if maybe the serpent was on to something. Seeing that they were circling the bait, the snake went all in. "Not only is it tasty", the snake said, "but if you eat it you will know everything that God knows!" Eve and Adam were convinced and so they ate. Ah ha! You may be thinking – "It's the snake's fault! It caused this!" No. It wasn't the snake's fault.

The greatest gift and responsibility God gave people was choice. To be able to choose to obey. Adam and Eve had a choice. Would they continually rely on and trust God for EVERYTHING, or did they want to take His place? Did they want to decide for themselves what was good and what was evil, or simply trust God?

When they saw that the forbidden fruit looked tasty and satisfying, they thought it would make them as wise as God. So they reached up with their own hand, took the fruit, put it to their mouth, and took a bite. That's right; it wasn't God's fault; it wasn't the serpent's fault. It was Adam's fault; it was Eve's fault. It was their choice. It was their pride. It was their death.

And so God searched them out in the garden, shared some words, shared some tears, promised them that the serpent's head would soon be crushed,[5] and sent them away as wanderers. The door to the Garden was closed, and now we wait for it to be reopened.

*Take time today to thank God for the ability to choose Him. Seek forgiveness where needed. Discuss the choices God has given you and how He helps you make wise choices.*

23

# NOAH

SU M TU W TH F SA

*But Noah found favor in the eyes of the LORD.*
*- Genesis 6:8 (NIV)*

I wish I could say that things got better between God and people. But things just got worse --- and worse --- and worse.

Outside the Garden, Adam and Eve had many children, and their children had children, and their children's children had – you guessed it – children! Soon the Earth was filled with people and these people forgot that there was a Garden. They forgot about the God who loves them and created them.

The people wandered farther and f a r t h e r and f a r t h e r from the special place God had made for them. Farther from the God who had made it all.

In fact, instead of being people who spent their time thinking about and talking to God, they became people whose every thought was only evil – ALL THE TIME!

Creation was broken. Adam took the first swing of the hammer and smashed the beautiful stained glass of Creation, and each generation after him took their turns swinging the hammer until there was nothing left but shards of glass, dust, and rubble. And so God lamented. He regretted. He wondered if He should have ever have made man and woman. God was troubled, but God still had a plan. He wouldn't discard all of creation; instead, He would restore it.

Humanity wouldn't be forever removed from God's presence. There would be a new land and a new kingdom. The relationship would be restored, but first, man's evil had to be dealt with.

God had a plan to destroy evil and save humanity. His plan involved Noah.

Noah found favor in the eyes of the LORD. Noah was righteous and blameless. God said to Noah, "Get your hammer and get to work. You need to build a giant ark. The world is going to be baptized in water,[6] but I will bring you and your family up out of it. You will be spared in the ark of protection."

So Noah did what God said. Day and night, until he was finished, Noah swung his hammer building the ark. And God, doing what He said He would, sent floodwaters. The water covered all of the earth and every living thing was destroyed. Everything was gone except Noah, his family, and the animals that God protected inside the ark.

When the water receded, the giant boat came to a rest and Noah and his family were finally able to get off the ark and start a new life together. Noah and his family gave thanks to God for what He had done. God painted the sky with a rainbow, promising Noah He would never have to worry about being destroyed by floodwaters again.

It was now Noah's job to fill the Earth, and Noah and his family lived happily ever aft....

Wait. You know better than that – you know that trouble lurks around every corner. The good news though, is that from Noah's descendants there will be another man, another hammer, another ark of protection. But for now, we wait.

*Is there something broken around your house? Take some time today and fix it and thank God that He takes the time to fix things that are broken. Discuss with your family the many ways God has been faithful, even when we are not.*

# BABEL

SU M TU W TH F SA

*As the people moved eastward, they found a plain in Shinar and settled there... Then they said "Come, let us build ourselves a city, with a tower that reaches to the heavens, so that we can make a name for ourselves; otherwise we will be scattered over the face of the whole earth."  - Genesis 11:4 (NIV)*

After the flood, Noah's sons had children. This new "first" family was on their way to fulfilling the command of God to multiply and fill the whole Earth.[7] Except, at some point, as the people moved eastward, they came to a plain in Shinar and they stopped – they settled there. They were no longer concerned about fulfilling the command of God to increase and fill the Earth. Instead, they settled for what they thought would be best. Rather than fill the Earth with the image of God, they wanted to make a name for themselves. They wanted to build their empire. They wanted to exalt themselves. They thought they were improving their situation but actually, they were settling.

I am sure they settled there for good reason. I am sure that they looked out into the distance and were fearful because they knew there were wild animals and difficult terrain ahead. But, even more frightening than the things they knew were out there, was the uncertainty. They did not know what scary and dangerous things were around the next bend. They did know what was here, on the plain in Shinar. So they settled there. They settled for safety.

I am sure they looked at all they had begun to acquire and were fearful that moving forward would mean leaving some things behind. They began to realize that complete obedience would mean sacrifice, and there were some sacrifices they were not willing to make. They knew if they stopped now, they could keep what they had acquired. On top of that, they could build a city with a tower and acquire even more. So they settled there. They settled for stuff.

I am sure they had a deep desire to be remembered, to leave their mark on the world, to have something to show for their life. As they came to the plain in Shinar, they thought this would be the perfect place to build a monument to their greatness. They thought to themselves, "We no longer have to wander about and be scattered over the Earth and be forgotten; we can make a name for ourselves!" So they settled there. They settled for status.

Left to their own devices, humanity would have pursued safety and missed opportunity. They would have clung to their stuff and have nothing. They would have sought status and lost identity. So God, in His mercy, brought judgment. He came down to them, confused their language, and scattered humanity all over the earth.

There would be no unified rebellion. There would be no monument to humanity. There would only be scattered people – separated from one another and separated from God. Hope was all but lost. How would these divided people once again be made one with one another and one with God? How would these rebellious people once again reflect the divine image?

There is no happy ending found in the story of the Tower of Babel, but we can be certain, "In all things God is working for good, annoyed by the stupidity of some, but swayed from His plan by none."[8] So for now, we wait.

*Is there any area of your life where you are settling? Has safety, stuff, or status become more important than obedience? Take some time today to remember what God has called you to do. Seek wisdom and strength from Him.*

# ABRAM

SU M TU W TH F SA

*So Abram went as the LORD had told him.*
*Genesis 12:4a (NIV)*

The people during the time of Babel refused to fill the Earth. They traded in trust, faithfulness, and obedience for prestige, possessions, and protection. At the close of that story, readers are left with a big question mark. If you didn't know what came next, it would seem as if God had finally given up on humanity. At the end of the story of the Tower of Babel, there was no hope offered, no rainbow in the sky. There was nothing but a scattered and rebellious people.

However, God still had a plan. When the time was right, His eyes searched the Earth for someone who would willingly obey the decree to be fruitful and multiply and fill the Earth. He searched across all the Earth and chose Abram.

The Lord spoke to Abram and said, "Leave your land and I will make you into a great nation, and all the people of the Earth will be blessed through you." This was God's original plan in the Garden – an Earth filled with His image-bearers. This was God's plan with Noah: an Earth filled with people who were blameless and faithful. This was the plan resisted at Babel. Now, God's plan continued with Abram. When Abram heard the command of the Lord, he did what his ancestors before him failed to do. Abram went as the Lord told him to. He didn't know where he was going; he simply went.

Abram went as God directed and held on to the promise that God would make him into a great nation. However, after a while Abram became concerned. He was not quite sure how he, a man without any children, who was getting older every day, would become a great nation. He was unsure of how he would take possession of the land God had promised him. Abram believed God, but it still seemed like what God had promised was impossible.

The word of the LORD came in a vision reassuring Abram of His promise. God instructed Abram to prepare a covenant ceremony which would create an unbreakable contract. Abram brought God a heifer, a goat, a ram, a dove, and a pigeon. He then cut the animals in half and lay them side-by-side. Abram did as God instructed, then he waited and waited. He waited so long that the mangled bloody mess in front of him attracted scavenger birds. Abram had to chase away these birds and then wait some more. Finally, Abram fell into a deep sleep. As he slept, God told Abram about the future of His people and assured Abram that they would one day live in the land that was promised.

To show He was serious about His promise, God passed through the dead, bloody, mangled animals; first as a smoking fire pot and then as a flaming torch. In Abram's time, this is how unbreakable covenants were made. After the terms were settled, each party would walk through the death and say, "If I do not fulfill the terms of this covenant, may what was done to these animals also be done to me."

There was something different about this covenant. God did not require Abram to walk through the death. In fact, Abram was sleeping when it happened! Only God walked through because this promise had nothing to do with Abram. The promise would be kept, not by Abram's strength or wisdom, but by God's. "When God made His promise to Abram, since there was no one greater for Him to swear by, He swore by Himself." [9]

God's faithfulness is unwavering. God keeps His promises even if He has to be killed and mangled, like the animals Abram placed on the ground before Him. God is faithful, so we patiently wait.

*What promises has God made to you? In what ways has God been faithful to you?*
*Are there any promises you have made that need to be kept?*

# ISAAC

SU M TU W TH F SA

*Abraham answered, "God himself will provide the lamb for the burnt offering, my son." And the two of them went on together.*
*-Genesis 22:8 (NIV)*

Abram waited patiently for God's promise to be fulfilled. God reminded Abram of His faithfulness by changing Abram's name to Abraham, which means father of many. Abraham waited and waited until at last, he and Sarah had a son. Their new son brought so much joy and laughter to them that they named him Isaac, which in Hebrew means laughter.

Abraham and Sarah did their best to raise Isaac in the ways of the LORD. Isaac was a good son who loved his parents and loved God. Isaac grew strong and became more and more able-bodied. It was around this time that God decided to test Abraham. God said to Abraham, "Take your son, your only son whom you love, and sacrifice him as a burnt offering."

Sacrifice your own son! Can you imagine? Imagine the sense of dread and terror that came over Abraham as he heard God's instructions. But Abraham reminded himself, "God is faithful and powerful." So Abraham reasoned, "God will raise Isaac from the dead, to keep His promise, if He has to! "[10]

The next morning Abraham loaded up his donkey, and he, Isaac, and two servants journeyed together to worship God. When they got closer to the place the

LORD had chosen, Abraham unloaded the donkey and instructed the servants to stay behind. Isaac carried the wood for the sacrifice while Abraham carried a torch and a knife. On the way up to the place of sacrifice, Isaac became curious and asked his dad, "Where is the lamb that we will sacrifice to the LORD?"

"Isaac, my son," Abraham replied, "The LORD will provide the sacrificial lamb." When they reached the chosen place, Abraham prepared the altar. The time came to place the sacrifice on the altar. Scripture does not record the conversation that took place between Abraham and Isaac, but perhaps it went something like this:

"Isaac, my son whom I love, please trust me, your father, as I trust God, our Father. God has requested you as a sacrifice." Isaac, after hearing the words of his father, put out his hands and was freely bound and placed on the altar.

Isaac lay still on the altar. Abraham began to lift his knife with a slight quiver in his hand. Just then, as Abraham lifted his knife to sacrifice his son, the angel of the LORD called out to stop him. Abraham's test was over. Abraham lifted his eyes and saw a ram stuck in the thicket.

God provided a ram that day to be sacrificed in place of Isaac. We wait for the day when the Lamb will be provided just as Abraham foretold.

*In what ways is our faith tested today? What can help us when our faith is tested? Pray for the strength you need to face each days challenges.*

# JACOB

SU M TU W TH F SA

*He took one of the stones here, set it under his head and lay down to sleep. And he dreamed: A stairway was set on the ground and it reached all the way to the sky; angels of God were going up and ...down.*
*—Genesis 28:11-12 (MSG)*

If there was ever a cunning, crafty, and calculating character in all of the Bible, it was Jacob. Jacob was the sneaky, scheming, sly younger son of Isaac and his wife Rebekah.  Jacob was just seconds younger than his twin brother Esau.

When Esau was born, his dad could already tell he was going to be a "manly man" because this newborn baby already had chest hair! Then there was Jacob; he was just a little ankle-biter. Or was it heel-grabber? When the two boys grew older, Esau lived up to expectations and became a great hunter. He would go out into the country to hunt down wild animals and bring the meat home for dad.

Meanwhile, Jacob stayed home. He was always under foot, clenching tightly to his mother's apron strings. This is just where Rebekah wanted him because she loved Jacob.

Jacob already had a scheme in mind. He knew of his older brother's favored position, and that his brother was in line to inherit much from his dad. So Jacob set out to grab hold of Esau's birthright. This was Esau's inheritance to give away or keep, and Jacob wanted to figure out a way to wrestle it out of Esau's hands.

One day when Esau came home from a hunt, he was exhausted. He was completely famished and dramatically exclaimed, "I am so hungry that I could die. Gimme some of that stew!" Jacob saw his opportunity and said, "Have I got a deal for you! I will give you all the stew you want in trade for your birthright!" Jacob took advantage of his brother's need. Jacob didn't have to force Esau or fight him for the inheritance. They simply traded – birthright for a bowl of stew.

To make matters worse, later, with the help of his mom, Jacob tricked his father into giving him the blessing that was intended for Esau! Jacob took everything from Esau. It seemed to Esau that Jacob had stolen his life, so Esau vowed to take his brother's life.

Jacob the schemer, seeking to save his own skin, fled. He fled so fast and so far he became fatigued. So he pulled up a nice comfy rock for a pillow and slept. As Jacob slept, God came to him in a dream. God didn't come to take advantage of Jacob in his exhausted and weakened state as Jacob did to Esau. Instead, God showed Jacob a ladder that reached heaven, with angels moving up and down the ladder. God reminded Jacob of a great promise.

This was a promise greater than Jacob's character flaws. A promise greater than the mistakes of his parents, greater than the threats of his brother. God promised Jacob that his descendants would live in the Promised Land. God promised that all the nations would be blessed through his descendants. And best of all, God promised Jacob to be with him always. When Jacob awoke, he dedicated that place to God and called it the Gate of Heaven.[11]

Jacob would still have a lot to learn after that night, but there would come a day when he stopped hanging onto the feet of others and instead, held tightly to the heart of God. He would no longer be known as the schemer, but as Israel – the one who wrestles God. [12]

The God of Abraham, Isaac and Jacob keeps His promises. As we wait for Christmas, we are waiting for the One in whom all promises are fulfilled, the true Gate of Heaven, the Son of Man upon whom the angels ascend and descend.[13]

*Has God changed your heart like he changed Jacob's? Are there any broken relationships that need mending? Spend some time talking to God today.*

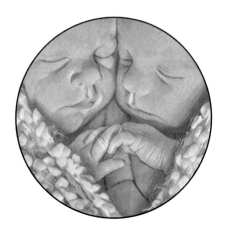

# TAMAR

*Judah got a wife for Er, his firstborn, and her name was Tamar.*
*– Genesis 38:6 (NIV)*

Jacob had twelve sons. One of these sons was named Judah. Judah married a Canaanite woman and had three sons named Er, Onan, and Shelah. When the time came for Er to be married, Judah found him a wife, a woman by the name of Tamar.

Tamar was a strong and beautiful young lady. As a child, we can imagine, she dreamed of the day when she would be married and have children of her own. That day had finally come. Judah and Tamar's father made an agreement that she would become the wife of Er. The wedding was a joyous and beautiful occasion, a celebration lasting many days.

Unfortunately the "honeymoon period" did not last for this new couple. Before Tamar had any children, Er's life of wickedness caught up to him and he died an early death. However, Tamar's hope for children was not lost. The custom of the day was for the next son to stand in for the deceased and give the widow children.[14] The next son was Onan.

Onan was expected to marry Tamar and give her children. Those children would carry on Er's name and legacy. Onan didn't want this. He wanted his own wife and his own children that would honor his own name. When Judah told him that he was to take Tamar as his wife, Onan became very upset because he knew that any children he had with her would not be considered his, but his older brother's. Onan married Tamar and slept with her, but he refused to give Tamar any children. Onan's life of wickedness caught up with him, and he too died.

Tamar again found herself without a husband and still without children. She still held onto hope, because Judah had another son. Judah, however, did not like the idea of giving yet another son to this woman. Judah was not quite sure what was going on, but he knew he didn't want to lose another son. So he lied to Tamar and made a promise that he never intended to keep. Judah told Tamar that when Shelah was older, he would give her the children she had been hoping and waiting for.

So Tamar waited, and waited, and waited, but Judah never honored his promise. It became clear to Tamar what was happening, so she made a plan. When Judah went on a business trip, Tamar disguised herself as a prostitute and went ahead of him and waited at the entrance to the city. She waited there, in disguise, until Judah went to her. Nine months later, Tamar gave birth to twins.[15]

This story is filled with lies, wickedness, and selfishness. It seems everyone involved was only and always concerned about themselves. Tamar was certainly a victim of selfish men, yet she also made poor decisions of her own. What a mess! Why tell this story? Can anything good come from all of this brokenness and sin?

Tamar's name will appear again in scripture in a genealogy alongside lots of other names. The genealogy of the one we are waiting for. A man about whom someone once asked, "Can anything good come from Nazareth?"[16]

*Share with someone today a story of when God took a messy situation and worked it out for His good. In your prayers remember to thank God for being able to redeem the ugliest of situations*

# JOSEPH

SU M TU W TH F SA

*You intended to harm me but God intended it for good to accomplish what is now being done, the saving of many lives. – Genesis 50:20 (NIV)*

Jacob had twelve sons. One of these sons was named Joseph. Jacob loved Joseph more than any of his sons. All of Joseph's brothers wore plain, old, regular, dirty work clothes, but Jacob bought for Joseph a beautifully colored and ornate robe -- the kind of robe you would never wear to work. Joseph's brothers saw how much more their dad loved him. They were hurt and became very jealous.

In their jealousy, they decided to get rid of Joseph. So when the time was right, that is exactly what they did. First, they captured Joseph and threw him into a deep pit. *PLUNK!* How terrifying it was for Joseph in the deep dark pit! He called out to his brothers, but no one answered. After a while, Joseph knew he had been in the pit too long for this to be a joke. He did not know what was happening, or if he would ever see his father again.

Just when Joseph was losing all hope of being freed, his brothers threw a rope down to him. As Joseph clung to the rope that would carry him to safety and saw shadows moving around at the top of the pit, relief swept over him. His fears of never seeing his father and mother again were easing. When he reached the top, we can imagine he thanked his brothers for setting him free. Perhaps he assured them he wouldn't tell their father what they had done.

Joseph finally made it out of the pit. He breathed in a deep breath of fresh air and stretched his arms out, glad to be free at last. Then, before he knew what was happening, he felt cold, metal chains around him. His eyes adjusted to the brightness just in time to see a stranger hand his brothers a small sack of money – 20 pieces of silver. He knew then he had been sold into slavery and would likely never see his family again.

Even though things got worse and worse for Joseph, he never lost his faith in God. When Joseph was falsely accused of a terrible crime, he didn't lose faith. When he was unjustly thrown into prison, he still remained faithful. When other prisoners he helped forgot about him, he remained faithful. Joseph walked through many, many difficult years, but in all of it, he never abandoned his faith in God.

Then one day, things changed for Joseph. This man, who had spent so long living in one pit after another, was called before the king of Egypt – Pharaoh. Pharaoh had had a troubling dream, but he didn't know what it meant. So in his desperation, Pharaoh called for a Hebrew slave that was serving a life term in prison. Pharaoh had heard that Joseph had the ability to interpret dreams. So Joseph humbly and confidently stood before the most powerful man in the world and, with the help of God, told him exactly what the dream meant. "Pharaoh," Joseph said, "there is going to be a famine. It is going to be bad, and you must prepare for it."

Pharaoh, seeing the wisdom of Joseph, appointed him his second-in-command over all of Egypt, and gave him the responsibility of preparing for the famine. For seven years, Joseph made preparations for the famine, and when the famine came, many were saved -- including Joseph's family.[17]

God's plan to save his people from famine began with a betrayal for a small bag of money. God's bigger plan to save humanity from sin was also in progress. And so, we wait for another who was betrayed for a small bag of money.

*Has the enemy ever meant to harm you but God worked it for good?*
*Thank God for being able to use difficult things for His glory.*

# MOSES

SU M TU W TH F SA

*"Go to Pharaoh and tell him... Release My people!"– Exodus 9:1 (NET)*

The sun rose over the desert of Midian as Moses went about the usual drudgery of shepherd life. The days of walking among the servants and treasures of Egypt were a shadow of a memory. Perhaps he contemplated the irony: "Back then, as a prince of Egypt, my every need was attended to, but nowadays I attend to the every need of these cattle." Perhaps he thought back with anger at the terrible enslavement of his people. Perhaps he missed the Egyptian woman who raised him, his Jewish mother, or his home. Perhaps he didn't think of them at all.

This day in the desert began like any other day: the sheep were being sheep, the sun above was hot, the air was dry. A desert bush was burning in the distance, barely noticeable. Happened all the time. Just a flicker in the distance. Soon, the dry branches would be consumed and the fire would burn out.

Several minutes later, Moses looked back toward the bush. It was still burning. He left the sheep behind to investigate. As he approached, his mind wandered through the possibilities: was this a campfire, or the start of a wildfire? Maybe a caravan of traders, or a group of bandits? Had disaster come to Midian?

When he finally had a good view, he found something very strange: a bush covered in flame but not burning up. It was on fire, but not consumed. He moved closer.

"Moses, Moses!" called a beautiful voice from the bush.

Stunned, all the man could say was, "Here I am."

The voice from the bush declared the Holy Presence: "The place you are standing is holy ground." Moses followed the instructions of the voice, and removed his shoes and stopped where he stood -- The beautiful voice spoke again.

"I AM – the God of Abraham, Isaac, and Jacob. I AM - Yahweh"[18]

This statement would shape the rest of Moses' life. The God of his forefathers, the God of Creation, had spoken to him. However, he had yet to discover who this God truly was. This truth would be revealed to Moses through the mission that God would send him on.

God sent Moses to confront Pharaoh. God had promised to be with Moses, but Moses knew that it would take more than the God of a bush to defeat the Egyptian king and his armies of soldiers and magicians. Moses sensed the power of God, but he needed more.

So that day at the bush, God showed just a portion of His power to Moses. He transformed a simple walking stick into a living snake, proving He had power over life and nature. God struck Moses with sores and healed him an instant later, proving His power to both strike and heal. God promised to send Aaron to assist Moses, proving He was a God who provided help. Neither Pharaoh, nor the pagan gods, nor their priests, nor prayers could withstand the might of the Holy One of Israel. Moses headed to Egypt.

\*\*\*

Nine times God struck Egypt. Each plague was more terrible than the last, but then came the tenth plague. This was the worst of them all. Pharaoh had taught his people that he was both god and king. God would prove Yahweh was God and King, even over Pharaoh. That night, Pharaoh's son was struck dead along with all the eldest sons of Egypt. The blood of a sacrificed lamb protected the Israelites from death. Pharaoh, now humbled, saw how far God would go to free His people.

Now we wait for the sacrificial Lamb of God that brings true freedom.

*What is true freedom that God brings? How has God shown you he is real and powerful? Spend some time praying today, preparing your heart for Him.*

# JOSHUA

SU M TU W TH F SA

*Did I not command you? Be strong and courageous! Do not fear or be dismayed, for Yahweh your God is with you wherever you go.*
*— Joshua 1:9 (LEB)*

The waters crashed down behind them. The miraculous pathway God opened for Israel slammed shut on those who were pursuing them. Pharaoh's oppression of the people of God had finally ended, and they were safe at last. A million people breathed a sigh of relief. Life would never look the same. They had moved into the desert called Sin under the faithful leadership of Moses.

Somewhere in this great migration of people was a young man named Joshua. He was strong and diligent. The miracles he witnessed in the wilderness, the supernatural provision of manna and quail, had forged in him faith and trust in God. His faith was one of the reasons Joshua became the right-hand man to Moses, groomed to take over the leadership for the next generation.

When the Israelites finally arrived at the border of their new home, God told Moses to send spies into the Promised Land. They were to scout out the land and return with a report. Twelve men were chosen for the job; one man from each tribe. Joshua was chosen to represent Ephraim.

For forty days, the twelve men traveled the land, exploring the wondrous things God was going to give them. The land flowed with milk and honey! They even saw clusters of grapes that were so big they had to be carried by two men!

When they returned with the report to Moses and the Israelites, the people were amazed by the wonderful things the men brought back. But when the spies began to speak, Joshua's mind filled with confusion and frustration.

The men spoke of giants and mighty warriors. They spoke of impenetrable fortified cities and they listed off the vast number of enemies. They said the ground itself would open up and devour them! Ten of the twelve men reported a hopeless situation. It all seemed impossible to those ten men.

Finally Caleb, the spy from the clan of Judah, spoke; a voice of faith and courage in a sea of chaos and fear. "Let's go conquer them now. Surely we will prevail!" Hope flickered in the back of Joshua's mind, but the people were afraid. They would rather return to slavery in Egypt than face the frightening foe ahead of them.

Joshua and Caleb tore their clothes and begged the people, "Don't you know who our God is? Trust Him for He is with us."

In spite of everything God had done for His people, their fear led them to rebel against God. They refused to take that which God had always planned to give them. Their fear, rebellion, and grumbling prevented them from entering the Promised Land. Instead, they would wander the desert called Sin for forty years.[19]

Joshua and Caleb alone would fearlessly lead the next generation to the Promised Land. Soon, someone is coming who calms all of our fears, one whose wonders exceed that of milk and honey and grapes.

*Today, is there anything that God wants to give you that fear prevents you from accepting? Pray God would fill you with His perfect love that casts out all fear.*

# RAHAB

SU M TU W TH F SA

> *"Shout! For the LORD has given you the city!.... Only Rahab the prostitute ... and her house shall be spared." – Joshua 6:16 (NIV)*

The people of God had wandered for a generation, stalled in the desert. Except for Joshua and Caleb, every one of them was born in the desert. They grew up parched by the sun, moving from place to place, constantly searching for a little water, and a little grass for the animals. They had heard the stories of the powerful God who smote Pharaoh with ten plagues, but none of them had seen it. They heard about the miracles, like the parting of Red Sea, but none of them had passed through it. They had heard the promise of a land flowing with milk and honey, but none of them had tasted it.

Finally that land of promise was before them. They could see the thing that God had told them to wait for. At last, the day they had waited for, expected, and prayed for was here, and they would win themselves a home. God was there, on their side, and nothing could stop them! No weapon forged against them would prosper, the battle belonged to the LORD. Let's go!

But then God said, "Wait a minute. First, send out some spies to check it out." I always imagine Joshua and Caleb face-palming. "God, haven't we been here before? If the people chicken out again, are we going to have wander for another forty years?"

Joshua sent out the spies as God commanded. The spies were almost captured and killed, but they were rescued by a woman named Rahab. She told them that the people in Jericho were melting in fear. Jericho's warriors were hiding behind their wall, shaking in their sandals, more likely to flee than fight.

Soon the army of Israel marched into Canaan. After wandering their whole lives, they entered the Promised Land and they knew they could take it. The enemy was weak, God is strong, and the Israelites are not looking too shabby! The young Israelite warriors were ready to run up and take the city. But God said... "Wait."

Wait?

"Before you can take the land, here is what I want you to do. Take your army, and march through the most dangerous area for battle. March around the walls, then blow your horns. Do that for six days, and then on the Sabbath, march seven times. I'll see you in a week."

The Israelites did exactly what God said to do. At the final trumpet blast, the city fell -- all except the house of Rahab. The spies had promised to spare her and her family, but they were under no obligation for anything else. They could have rejected Rahab, sent her away. They had every reason to do so.

They could have rejected her because she was a sinner.
   ...because she was an unclean pagan woman.
   ...because she was a foreign enemy.
   ...because she was a traitor.
   ...because she was broken, hopeless, and helpless.
   ...because she had nothing to offer.

Thanks be to God, He accepts us just as we are.

The Israelites accepted Rahab as well. She married a man named Salmon. They had a son named Boaz. And from this family, we wait for the one who will be a friend to all hopeless and broken people, the one who declares his victory with a trumpet blast!

*Have you felt like an outsider with the People of God? Pray, remembering that God accepts us, broken pieces and all.*

# JUDGES

SU M TU W TH F SA

*Joshua son of Nun, servant of Yahweh, died.... another generation grew up after them who did not know Yahweh or the work he had done for Israel. – Judges 2:8-10 (LEB)*

During the days of Joshua, the Israelites were enjoying great success. God was faithful to them and they were faithful to God. The Israelites were winning victory after victory, and God's promise was fulfilled. They were living in the land of promise, the land flowing with milk and honey. It couldn't get any better than this.

Then Joshua died.

Then all the leaders of Israel died.

The children became adults – and this new generation did not know God or the great things He had done. Their parents, in all their successes and all their victories, forgot the most important thing. They forgot to teach their children the ways of God.[20]

It wasn't long until the Israelites turned from God, chased after idols, and did evil. They were not faithful to God. So God, who had led them into victory time and time again, decided to no longer drive the enemies of Israel out of the land. The Israelites who were once victorious were now servants of their enemy.

They were under the control of their enemy for eight years until they finally learned their lesson and turned back to God, calling out for help. God heard their prayers and sent a man named Othniel to deliver them from the hands of their enemy.

Israel had learned their lesson and remained faithful to God, right?.... NOPE!

Again and again and again, Israel turned their back on God and chased after idols. Each time, God allowed their enemies to defeat them, and each time, God sent help when they asked for it. They sinned, their enemies defeated them, and they repented, so God sent Ehud. They sinned, their enemies defeated them, they repented, and God sent Shamgar. Then God sent Deborah, then Gideon, then Tola, then Jair.

Now, they finally learned their lesson right? ....... NOPE!

God had to send Jephthah, Ibzan, Elon, Abdon, Samson....this went on for hundreds of years! The Israelites were caught in a tragic cycle. They wanted God to be their savior, but what they needed was for God to be their King. However, they had no king and everyone did as they saw fit.

God's plan was at work. He was sending a Savior and a King for Israel and all of humanity. It is on Him that we now wait.

*Have you ever been stuck in a vicious cycle? God forgave the Israelites whenever they asked. Is there someone you need to forgive today?*

# RUTH

SU M TU W TH F SA

*May your family become like the family of Perez—whom Tamar bore to Judah— through the descendants the L<small>ORD</small> gives you by this young woman. – Ruth 4:12 (NET)*

In the midst of the chaos that defined the time of the Judges, when the descendants of Israel were stuck in a cycle of sin, destruction, repentance, and salvation, there was a family from Bethlehem. A man, his wife, and their two sons were struggling to survive in Bethlehem because there was a famine.

The man loved his family, and was worried because they had no food. So, not knowing what else to do, he moved his family to a foreign land: Moab, the land of their enemies. They wouldn't fit in and would have no friends, but they would have food. They would survive – or so he thought.

While living in Moab, the man died, leaving Naomi, his widow, and her two sons. This wasn't the picture-perfect life Naomi wanted, but she was making it work. Her sons soon found wives in Moab and things began looking up. Naomi grew close to her sons' wives, Orpah and Ruth. It started to feel like a family again. They would be okay – or so she thought.

While living in Moab, Naomi's two sons died. Naomi was getting older and she had no way to support herself. Her husband was gone, her sons were gone, and she had nothing to offer her daughters-in-law. Naomi decided to do the best thing for everyone involved. She would go back home and leave Orpah and Ruth in Moab to find new husbands. But Ruth loved Naomi very much and clung to her. Ruth refused to leave her, so the two went back to Bethlehem together. The past seemed bitter and the future bleak – or so they thought.

The two women returned to Bethlehem at the beginning of harvest season. Ruth went to the fields to pick up the scraps that were dropped, hoping it would be enough to feed herself and Naomi. In those days, the poor were allowed to gather the leftovers after the workers had finished harvesting the field. This is how they would survive.[21] Gathering other people's leftovers. This would be her life now – or so she thought.

While Ruth was working, the field owner, Boaz, son of Rahab, came home. Boaz saw Ruth scavenging for leftovers in his fields and was moved with compassion. Ruth's beauty and dedication moved him with love. He instructed his servants to treat her with great kindness; to let her drink when she was thirsty, and to purposely drop sheaves of grain for her to glean. Their love for one another grew. Ruth wanted to marry Boaz, and Boaz wanted to marry Ruth. But Boaz knew there was another man who had rights to marry Ruth, and he would never forfeit his claim. Boaz couldn't marry her – or so he thought.

Boaz went to work. He wanted to redeem Ruth, to make her his wife. He called the elders together. He summoned the man that had rights. Boaz presented the information to the elders and to this man. If this was going to be done, Boaz wanted to make sure it was done correctly. To Boaz's delight, and possible surprise, the one that could have taken Ruth to be his wife allowed Boaz and Ruth to marry. There was a great wedding celebration with an extravagant feast. Soon, Boaz and Ruth would have a son named Obed. Obed would later have a son named Jesse. The days of chaos will soon be over.

Sometimes when things seem good, they can turn bad quickly. Sometimes when the future seems bleak, we are surprised by love. When we realize that we are spiritual beggars, redemption comes. We are expecting the arrival of the one that will bring redemption and fill the bellies of beggars with the bread of life. We are one day closer, but for now, we wait.

*Ruth's loyalty and friendship echoed throughout time. What can you do to have a positive impact on those around you today? To whom can you show friendship?*

47

# SAUL

SU M TU W TH F SA

*But the people refused to listen to Samuel. "No!" they said. "We want a king over us. Then we will be like the other nations, with a king to lead us...and fight our battles." – 1 Samuel 8:19-20 (NIV)*

After more than four hundred years of being governed by judges, the people were eager to be ruled by a king. The prophet Samuel warned them that a king would send their children into battle, tax the best of their produce, and rule them with a heavy hand. Samuel warned that choosing a human king was to reject God. Yet, the people persisted, and God gave them a king. His name was Saul.

***

One day, Saul's dad sent him out to find some donkeys that had wandered off. Saul and his servant were not able to find the animals. So they decided to seek out Samuel. Maybe God's prophet could tell them where the donkeys were.

When they arrived, Saul immediately found Samuel, and got much more than he bargained for. Samuel, the seer,[22] sat Saul at the honored place of the banquet. This banquet was prepared for Saul before he even knew he was going to the prophet's house! Samuel told Saul that all of Israel had hung its hopes on him and on his family.

As the sun rose, Saul and his servant headed home. As they started their journey, the prophet stopped Saul to speak with him privately. It was there, at an unremarkable place, somewhere on the outskirts of the city, that Saul was anointed as the first king of God's people. God gave Saul a new heart that day, but when Saul returned home, he acted like nothing had happened.

Some time after Saul had returned home, Samuel came to town to reveal who the king would be. Samuel called all the families of Israel together to cast lots.[23] First, the lot fell to the tribe of Benjamin, then to Saul's family. Finally, it fell to Saul. But where was Saul? He was hiding in the baggage! For a second time, young Saul was declared king. There were many who thought that this boy was totally unfit to be king. Saul agreed with them, and so when he returned home he didn't do anything to secure his position as king. Instead, he went to the fields to plow. What would it take for him to act like a king?

***

Jabesh-Gilead, a town of the half-tribe of Manasseh, was besieged by a vicious warlord called Nahash the Ammonite. The people had no hope of defending themselves against the invaders, so they bargained for peace. "Give us seven days to find help, then we will surrender to you."

Nahash gave them seven days, but promised that when he returned, he would gouge out the right eye of every man. Nahash was confident that no one would help them. Surely, there was no one in all of Israel that would stand up to him. What he didn't know, however, was that the anointed king, Saul, was nearby in a field.

When word of Nahash's threats reached Saul, he was furious and sprang to action. Saul sent word across the nation to follow him into battle. When the time came, 330,000 men joined to fight with Saul. They attacked the Ammonite invaders, and Saul had his first great victory. That day, Saul went from farmer to king. A third time, Saul is made king, and this time it sticks.

At first, Saul served God well as king, but greed and rebellion slipped into his heart. Eventually, sin drove a wedge between Saul and God. In time, the kingdom was taken from him and given to another. Saul was an uncertain and unstable king, appointed over a people that had difficulty trusting God. Saul's leadership was temporary.

Another leader is coming, a sure foundation, whose reign will never end. He will lead us into God's presence. For Him, we wait.

*Have you been unsure about God's calling? Have you been unfaithful to the call? Pray for your leaders today; that God would impart, in them and in you, confidence..*

# JESSE

SU M TU W TH F SA

*A shoot shall come out from the stump of Jesse, and a branch shall grow out of his roots. The Spirit of the LORD shall rest on him.*
*– Isaiah 11:1-2a (NRSV)*

God rejected Saul as king of Israel. Saul had the appearance of a king, but his heart was filled with pride and foolishness. It was time for God to appoint a new king for Israel. God sought out someone who ran after His own heart, and He found just who He was looking for -- a young man living in the city of Bethlehem, from the family of Jesse. God told His prophet Samuel to go visit Jesse's family and anoint the appointed one as the future king of Israel.

Samuel understood that going to anoint a new king while Saul was still king was dangerous. Samuel could be killed. To protect Samuel, God told him to take a heifer with him and use the trip as an opportunity to sacrifice to the LORD. Samuel did as the LORD instructed and went to Bethlehem to make a sacrifice. Samuel invited Jesse and his family to the occasion. This was his opportunity to find the one from Jesse's family that would be king.

Right away, Jesse's oldest son caught the eye of Samuel. He was tall and kingly-looking. Surely this was a king the people would accept – this had to be God's chosen one. But the LORD told Samuel, "This is not the king. Outwardly he may look like the perfect candidate, but God looks at the heart."

"If it is not my eldest son, then perhaps the next eldest," thought Jesse. He presented his next son to the prophet. This was not the king. So Jesse tried the next son, but the third son was not to be king, either. This didn't make sense. If these three were not to be the next king, then who? These three knew war and what it meant to fight. They knew what it meant to be good soldiers. They were faithful to Saul.[24] If not these three, then who?

One by one, Jesse presented his sons to the prophet of God, and one by one they were rejected as the next king of Israel. Seven sons presented. Seven sons rejected. Had God changed His mind? Was He mistaken? Samuel knew God was faithful, and if God said the next king would be one of Jesse's sons, then the next king would be one of Jesse's sons. So Samuel asked, "Do you have any other sons?"

Yes, there was another son. But he was the youngest. He was insignificant. He wasn't even invited to the sacrifice. He was forgotten in the fields with the sheep.

"Go get him," Samuel instructed.

After some time passed, in walked David, the shepherd. David, the one who was faithful to God.[25] David, the one who chased after God's heart. This was the one. Samuel had found the one God had appointed. There was only one thing left to do -- anoint him, then wait. So Samuel took his horn of oil and poured it over David's head, anointing him the next king of Israel.

From that day forward, the Holy Spirit was upon David in great power. David would become the greatest king Israel would ever see. But after David comes the greatest King the world will ever know. It is upon Him that we wait.

*David to his family was invisible, forgotten, and insignificant. Have you ever felt invisible or insignificant? Where do we find our true significance? To whom are we never invisible? Pray for the invisible and the outcasts today.*

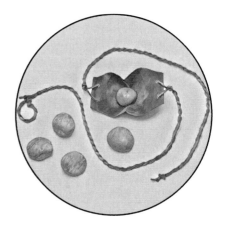

# DAVID

SU M TU W TH F SA

*Create in me a clean heart, O God; and renew a right spirit within me. Cast me not away from thy presence; and take not thy holy spirit from me. Restore unto me the joy of thy salvation; and uphold me with thy free spirit. – Psalm 51:10-12 (KJV)*

David: the greatest king Israel would ever know. David's fame and victories are well-known. Even after thousands of years, we still share stories of his conquests. His most famous battle of all, though, happened before he became king. He was a shepherd boy when he stood toe-to-toe with a giant, a Philistine named Goliath.

Goliath was a massive man. He stood almost ten feet tall -- 9'9", to be exact. He was well-armored and well-armed. He was an experienced warrior. All of the Israelites feared him; all of them thought their situation was hopeless. Every day, Goliath went out to the battlefield and mocked them and challenged them. No one responded. Even King Saul, who was a head and shoulder taller than most men, would not stand up to him.

But David did. David wasn't a warrior; he had no place on the battlefield. However, when David walked into camp and heard Goliath mocking God and His people, he knew something must be done. So he took his sling. He gathered five smooth stones and did what no one else would: he met Goliath on the battlefield.

And the giant fell!

Years later, after David had become king, he faced another battle. In the spring, when the kings would go off to war, David stayed home, far from where men fought with shields and swords. But David would face something far more deadly. He was going to battle with sin, and he would lose.

As David walked around his palace, he looked out to the horizon and noticed on a nearby rooftop a beautiful woman; a married woman. The wife of one of his best and most loyal soldiers. But David wasn't a soldier. He was the king, and he could take whatever he wanted. So he did. He summoned the woman, the wife of Uriah. Her name was Bathsheba.

Bathsheba became pregnant and David was afraid his sin would be discovered. So David, not wanting to be discovered, did the unthinkable and had Uriah killed. David, the man after God's heart. David, the giant killer, was now David, the adulterer and murderer.

David was able to overcome the most powerful of external forces, but he couldn't conquer the sin within his heart. He knew he had grieved the Spirit of God. He felt like he was drifting away. And so, when David was confronted with his sin, he prayed:

> *Create for me a pure heart, O God! Renew a resolute spirit within me!*
> *Do not reject me! Do not take your Holy Spirit away from me!*
> *Let me again experience the joy of your deliverance!*
> *Sustain me by giving me the desire to obey!*
> Psalm 51:10-12 (NET)

His heart was free. His heart chased God. His descendant would always be on the throne.[26] It is for that descendant, the king in the line of David, who cleanses hearts, that we wait.

*Is God the king of your heart? Does your heart need cleansed? Thank God for His forgiveness and consecrate your heart to Him.*

# SOLOMON

SU M TU W TH F SA

> *"May your eyes be open day and night toward this house, the place where you promised to set your name, and may you heed the prayer that your servant prays towards this place.... Likewise when foreigners, who are not of your people Israel...come and pray toward this house, may you hear from heaven your dwelling place... in order that all the people of the earth may know your name and fear you."*
> *— 2 Chronicles 6:20,32,33 (NRSV)*

King David and Bathsheba lost their first son, but they would have another. His name was Solomon and he would be king. Solomon was one of the great kings of Israel because God was with him.

One night, God appeared to Solomon and said, "Solomon, ask me for anything you want, and it will be yours!" Wow! Can you imagine that? What would you ask for? Most would ask for fame or fortune. Perhaps some would use the opportunity to get revenge or to erase a past mistake. Maybe you would ask God for a long life. But not Solomon-- he asked for something different.

Solomon looked at the task that lay before him. He was king. He was responsible for leading God's people. How could he do that effectively? How could anyone?! If he was going to be a good king, there was one thing he would need more than anything. Solomon would need wisdom. He didn't need lots of money, or fame. He didn't need a stockpile of trivial information. He needed wisdom. He needed the wisdom that begins with the fear of the LORD. He needed to know what to do, how to do it, and to have the strength to do it.

So Solomon said, "God, the job I have before me is great, and above all else I need wisdom in order to lead your people effectively."

"Solomon," God replied, "your request is wise. And because you did not ask for meaningless things like fame and fortune, but for something as valuable as wisdom, not only will I give you wisdom, but I will also give you wealth and honor among all people."

God was true to His word, and Solomon became the wealthiest of all the kings that had ever lived. He had more chariots, more cattle, more gold, silver, and precious stones than anyone. Solomon had access to all the stones and hardwood he needed for building. When it came to material possessions, he wanted for nothing, but more important than this, he also had great wisdom. His wisdom was so great that leaders would travel very long distances to witness it and to learn from him.

All the great wealth and wisdom that was granted him by God would serve a great purpose. Solomon, led by God, took the plans given to him by his father David and constructed the Temple. Israel now had a central place of worship, a monument to the glory of Yahweh. It was a place Israelites could go to encounter God, because in the center of the Temple was the Ark of the Covenant, the place where God's presence resided. This Temple would be a house of prayer for the nations and all people. Even foreigners would be able to look to it and bring requests to Israel's God. All the nations of the earth would be blessed.

King Solomon was the last king of a united Israel. After his reign, the kingdom split and fell into turmoil. The Temple would continue to be a treasure to the people for centuries, but even the Temple proved to be temporary. There is one coming who will reestablish an eternal Temple. He will unite all people. He is the embodiment of wisdom. But for now, we wait.

*Is there something for which you need wisdom? Pray for God's wisdom today with confidence He will give it.*

# ELIJAH

SU M TU W TH F SA

*"See, I will send the prophet Elijah to you before that great and dreadful day of the LORD comes. He will turn the hearts of the parents to their children, and the hearts of the children to their parents." - Malachi 4:5-6a (NIV) spoken 400 years after Elijah*

King Ahab began his reign about half a century after the death of King Solomon. The once-united kingdom was now split in two: the nation of Israel in the North, and Judah in the South. The descendants of Abraham had fallen far from the will of God, and King Ahab turned the rebellion up a notch. He considered sin to be a trivial matter and placed his loyalty and worship upon Baal. King Ahab even had the nerve to build a temple in Samaria that was dedicated to the worship of Baal. Things were looking bad in Israel.

So God raised up a prophet. Elijah spoke boldly to the king and the rest of the nation. He faithfully delivered God's warnings and verdicts against them. It seemed he was the only faithful one left in all of Israel. Elijah stood alone. Elijah stood with courage. He challenged the prophets of Baal. Elijah would demonstrate that it was Yahweh, and not Baal, that was the one true God.

Elijah and the prophets of Baal met on Mount Carmel. Each set up an altar. The stage was set; everyone would now see the power of Yahweh. The god that answered with fire would be the victor. The prophets of Baal danced about crying out to their god. This went on for hours, but the bawling Baal-ites had no luck. The show the prophets of Baal put on amused Elijah. He mocked them saying, "What is the matter? Perhaps your god is taking a bathroom break!"

Hours and hours passed, and still no response from Baal. Elijah stood. It was his turn. But first he had a point to make, so Elijah doused his altar with buckets and buckets of water. When the altar was dripping wet, the prophet of Yahweh lifted his hands to heaven and prayed. Then...

WHOOOOOOSH! The LORD God answered with fire.

God had won. Elijah was seen to be in the right, the true prophet of God. However, this victory did not bring the joy it should have. Elijah became very depressed. He, after all, was still the only one faithful to God. He was all alone. Elijah went to hide. He was tired. He was done.

In his depression, God came. "Elijah, you are not alone and you still have a job to do. Get up and anoint the next king, anoint the next prophet, and take heart, because there is a remnant. There are 7,000 people who have remained faithful to me."

Elijah is one of the most famous prophets in the Bible. After these events, he would be taken to heaven in a chariot of fire, not having to face death. God would continue to preserve his treasure through a remnant in each generation, but Israel would not repent. Evil king after evil king would come, and God would send prophets to warn them; men like Amos, Hosea, Micah, Nahum, and Isaiah. Evil kings and righteous prophets spanned 150 years. God was patient, but it became time for Israel to face the consequences of their actions. Yahweh, the God of Israel, allowed the nation of Assyria to conquer the northern kingdom. Israel fell. Now, only the two tribes in the Kingdom of Judah remained.

This was a sad time for the children of Abraham, and things were going to get worse. But the lights of hope, love, and joy still flicker; and peace is prophesied. Four hundred years after Elijah, there came a prophet that foretold of Elijah's return.[27] He will indeed return as a voice calling out in the wilderness, preparing the way for the one we wait for.

*Have you remained faithful to God or does your loyalty lay elsewhere? Have you ever felt alone? Pray for God to reveal any idols in your life, and for the strength to abandon them. Look for opportunities to get involved at your local church.*

# JONAH

SU M TU W TH F SA

*"That is why I fled to Tarshish at the beginning; for I knew that you are a gracious God and merciful, slow to anger, and abounding in steadfast love, and ready to relent from punishing." – Jonah 4:2b (NRSV)*

Jonah was a prophet. A reluctant prophet…. this is his story.

God spoke to Jonah one day and said, "Go to Nineveh and warn them of their wickedness."

Jonah hated the Ninevites. They were a cruel and vicious people. They worshipped idols and were great enemies of the Israelites. They were the terrorists of the day and if Jonah went to Nineveh, he could be killed because he would be an Israelite in a foreign land. Oh, how the Ninevites would punish him if he delivered this message of doom from God!

Jonah didn't go to Nineveh, but it wasn't because he was concerned for his own safety. Jonah had another reason.

Jonah ran in the opposite direction. He left the safety of Israel and got on a boat headed to a foreign land, a place that was far from Nineveh – Tarshish. But the boat wouldn't make it to its destination because God sent a great and terrible storm. The storm God sent was so violent that the weather-worn, professional sailors were scared for their lives. The sailors scurried about the ship, throwing over precious cargo, each one praying to his god to save them. All the while, Jonah slept because being in a violent storm was better than being in Nineveh. Surely this storm would pass -- but it didn't pass. Jonah realized that if he was going to escape God, he had to run farther away.

Jonah told the sailors to throw him overboard. They were reluctant at first because they didn't want any harm to befall their fellow traveler. But because Jonah insisted, the sailors threw Jonah into the sea and the storm was calmed.

Jonah sank and sank and sank to the bottom of the sea, to the very foundations of the Earth. He was now at the farthest place from God he could think to go. As his body struggled for air, Jonah thought, "Maybe Nineveh would be better than a watery grave. Maybe God would still remember his prophet."

With his last breath, Jonah let out a gurgle. It was a pathetic cry for help, but it was all Jonah could muster. Then, just as Jonah's life was ebbing away, he was enclosed by warmth. The watery grave was gone. He was alive! It was dark and cramped, and it still smelled like the bottom of the sea, but he was alive. Jonah, grateful that God had spared his life, gave thanks to God.

Jonah spent three days in this dark, cramped space when suddenly he was forcefully expelled onto dry ground. Jonah looked out to the sea just in time to see the instrument of his salvation -- a giant fish that God had sent.

God again spoke to Jonah and said, "Go to Nineveh and warn them of their sin." Jonah went to Nineveh and preached the shortest sermon in history. The people of the city repented and were saved! This was great news for Jonah, right?

But Jonah, who was so happy that God had saved him, was furious that God saved the 120,000 Gentiles in the city of Nineveh! This was why he had never wanted to go to Nineveh. He didn't want God to spare them!

Jonah was a self-centered, reluctant prophet who had to sink to the foundation of the Earth before he obeyed. We now wait for the selfless prophet, who, before the foundation of the world, was at the ready.

*Is your love for others more like Jonah's or God's? Are you walking in the direction God instructs? Pray for discernment and for God to fill your heart with His love.*

# JEREMIAH

SU M TU W TH F SA

*This is the brand-new covenant that I will make with Israel when the time comes. I will put my law within them – write it on their hearts! – and be their God. And they will be my people. – Jeremiah 31:33 (MSG)*

The people's hearts were still hard toward God. Witnessing the fall of their brothers to the north should have gotten their attention, but it didn't. God's people still rebelled against Him. So God continued to send prophets to His people. One such prophet was Jeremiah.

Jeremiah was called to be Judah's prophet when he was a young man. The thought of speaking to people was at first overwhelming for the young prophet. He did not understand how he, a youth, could speak for the eternal, everlasting God. But it was simple. The God who had called him would be with him. The God who appointed him to be a prophet would put His words in Jeremiah's mouth. Jeremiah would be the prophet of God. He would go where God sent, and he would say what God commanded.

Jeremiah was full of fire and emotion. He cried out against the sins of his people and warned them time and time again of the judgment that was to come. God revealed to Jeremiah that the people would be taken captive, removed from their home, and brought to Babylon. Not only this, but when they were conquered, Jeremiah told them, Jerusalem and the Temple would be destroyed. The Temple that Solomon built was supposed to be a place of hope for Jew and foreigner alike, a house of prayer for all nations. But the monument to Israel's faith would be destroyed and become a monument of ridicule.

Delivering such a message was difficult for Jeremiah. He loved his people, and the thought of them suffering under judgment caused him anguish and brought him to tears. Jeremiah pleaded to God to show mercy on His people. Knowing what was to come tore Jeremiah apart on the inside. Nevertheless, he preached because he knew it would be shameful and unhelpful to put a Band-Aid on a fatal wound, and to declare peace when their path was one of turmoil.[28]

Babylon was coming. Exile was coming. Destruction was coming, and it would overtake them because they had broken the law of God. Yet even though judgment was to come, there was still a flicker of hope. There was still a sparkle of joy. There would be a future peace because Yahweh, the God of Israel, loves His people greatly.

Because of this great love, God spoke to Jeremiah and he prophesied. Jeremiah said the exile would be temporary; it would only last 70 years. Then there would come the righteous branch of David.[29] There would come a new and improved covenant, a covenant where God would write His law on the hearts of His people. This covenant would not be like the old one. God would remove the rebellion from their hearts, and they would truly know Him.

And now we wait for the one, the branch of David, who will establish and seal this new covenant.

*How has God shown His love to you? Spend some time praying for those around you as Jeremiah prayed for the people of Israel.*

# DANIEL

SU M TU W TH F SA

*My God sent his angel and closed the lions' mouths so that they have not harmed me, because I was found to be innocent before him.*
*– Daniel 6:22 (NET)*

The people of God were displaced; captured and taken to Babylon. Nebuchadnezzar, king of Babylon, selected all the "best people." The good-looking, young, and intelligent men were selected for a three-years'- long education at the palace.[30] They would learn literature, language, science, culture, and even religion; all of it from the perspective of their Chaldean conquerors. These young men were given new names and new identities.

Among those taken were four young Jewish boys. They were highly blessed by the true God, and they rose to prominence in the palace. Daniel, their leader, was able to interpret the king's dreams. Due to this special insight, Daniel was given total governance over the country surrounding Babylon. His friends, Hananiah, Mishael, and Azariah, were also appointed to various positions of power.

Their faithful service often led Nebuchadnezzar to give glory to God, but as soon as he spoke well of Yahweh, he would turn around and offend Him. His first great offense to God was constructing an idol of himself. Nebuchadnezzar demanded that all in the kingdom worship the great-golden-monument to his foolish pride.

Hananiah, Mishael, and Azariah would not bow to the great-golden-nothing. They were brought before the king, and he again demanded their worship. When the three refused, he threatened to kill them by fire. The three men responded to the king with dread and boldness all at once:

"We don't have to answer for this because we've done nothing wrong. If you insist on this action, our God is able to save us. Even if He chooses to let His servants die, we will only worship the one true God."

Nebuchadnezzar threw himself into a violent rage, demanding that the heat of the furnace be made seven times hotter. The furnace was so hot that it killed the soldiers when they bound the three Jewish men with their own clothes and threw them in. The king watched with hate-filled eyes, expecting to see the three Jews burn. But he couldn't believe what he saw: there were not three burned-up corpses, but four men walking around. The king called for them and the three men came out. They didn't even smell like smoke!

*** 

After the Babylonians lost power, the Persians took control and Daniel found himself to be in service to a new king – Darius. King Darius wisely appointed qualified men, called satraps, to help him rule over his kingdom. Daniel found favor with Darius, and the satraps had to answer to him. This made the satraps jealous, so they tricked Darius to pass an unchangeable law: for thirty days, everyone in the kingdom could pray only to Darius. Anyone who prayed to another would be fed to the lions.

Daniel was not deterred, and he continued his practice of praying every day to God. The jealous satraps seized this opportunity and demanded King Darius throw Daniel into the den of lions. Daniel was in the den of hungry lions all night, but God miraculously saved him!

Daniel went on to receive visions of many things, including visions about the one who is to come -- the one on whom we are waiting.

*Have there been times you were ashamed of your faith? What stops you from praying openly like Daniel? Find someone to pray with today and find some to share your faith with. Pray and thank God for the courage He gives.*

# EZRA

SU M TU W TH F SA

*During the first year of the reign of king Cyrus of Persia, the LORD fulfilled Jeremiah's prophecy.... "Cyrus, king of Persia, hereby announces that Jehovah, the God of Heaven that gave me my vast empire, has now given me the responsibility of building him a temple in Jerusalem, in the land of Judah." – Ezra 1:1-2 (TLB)*

The exile in Babylon was a dangerous time for the Jews, but God provided for and protected them again and again. Assyria, Babylon, and finally Medeo-Persia had ruled over them. God's providence worked it out that Daniel was given authority in both Babylon and Persia. God used the powerful pagan emperors to bring Himself glory and bless His people.

At the same time, away from the capitals of powerful nations, in the forsaken ruin of Jerusalem, God again provided for His people. When power shifted from Babylon to Persia, He moved on the heart of the Persian King Cyrus to allow the Jews to return to their homeland. They could rebuild their city, their walls, and most importantly, the Temple. Even the sacred utensils that had been looted from the Temple were returned.

Tens of thousands of people gathered in the city, both those who lived in the land and those who had returned from Babylon. They gave gifts of gold and silver, and even priestly garments. They reestablished the priesthood, one group with the descendants of Aaron, and another that included all the Levites.

First, they built the altar where the priests would make sacrifices for their sin. Restarting the sacrificial system was their first priority, for it was their only way of connecting to God. You see, sin separates mankind from God, and sin can only be dealt with by blood. The blood of the beasts couldn't wash away sin for long, so the sacrifices could never stop. They would need a perfect sacrifice to truly defeat the pain and penalty of sin.

Then they began to build the Temple around the altar. As the Temple approached completion, the new generation jumped with joy and shouted, but the old men wept. This new Temple was so much less than what the old men remembered, but so much more than the young ones ever hoped for. How frustrating it must have been for all of them when Cyrus' grandson Artaxerxes stopped the work.

Politics would delay the building effort for many years, but bit by bit, the city and its walls were rebuilt. Eventually, they had to carry weapons as they worked, since so many of their neighbors tried to stop them.

Every time man tried to interfere, God would again help the process. In fact, it was in response to opposition that Ezra was sent to lead the rebuilding effort.

Eventually both the Temple and the wall would be restored. This Second Temple would be renovated and expanded again by Herod the Great. It is in that Temple that the one we are waiting for would walk, teach, and preach.

*The story of the Jewish people is a story of perseverance. Be encouraged today to keep moving forward even when things seem impossible. God will make a way. Spend some time praying for one another and the challenges you are facing.*

# ESTHER

SU M TU W TH F SA

*"And who knows* but that *you have come to your royal position for such a time as this?"* - *Esther 4: 14b (NIV)*

He was the most powerful man in the world. He was the wealthiest man in the world. He could have what he wanted, when he wanted it, and no one dared to defy him. His name was King Xerxes, the king of the Persians – the world power of the day.

King Xerxes, to demonstrate his wealth and his power, threw a party for all the nobles and officials. To show them that he had the most beautiful wife in the world, Xerxes ordered his wife to come and parade around before all the guests. However, his wife, Queen Vashti, did not want to be turned into a trophy. She was insulted that her husband would disgrace her like this. So the queen did what no one ever dared to do. She told the king, "NO!"

Vashti paid for her disobedience. Her crown was cruelly taken, and she was banished from the kingdom.

The loneliness of the nights caught up to Xerxes and he soon missed having a wife. But for the king, the most powerful man in the world, this was an easy problem to fix. King Xerxes commanded that all the young and beautiful women of the kingdom be brought before him so he could pick out a new wife.

All the women were gathered and, of all of them, there was one that stood out among the rest, a young lady named Esther. She was the most beautiful woman, and her poise and grace made her the perfect choice as the next queen of Persia.

But Esther had a secret; she was a Jew. This little detail could have prevented her from becoming queen, or could have been dangerous for her. So Esther, as instructed by her uncle Mordecai, kept this secret to herself.

***

He was the second most powerful man in the world. It was customary that people would kneel to him and pay him honor. It was unheard of for someone to defy him. His name was Haman, the king's most honored noble. As he went out of the palace one day, all the nobles and officials did indeed bow. All except one; Mordecai, Esther's uncle. Mordecai refused to bow because Mordecai was a Jew and he would only bow to God.

This infuriated Haman. He knew that something must be done. Mordecai must pay; not only Mordecai, but all of the Jewish people. They all needed to be punished! So Haman, the snake that he was, put into motion a plan to eliminate Every......... Last..............Jew.

***

Esther was the wife of the most powerful man in the world, certainly a role that had some benefits and put her in a special position. But she was still just a woman, and she was still just one of the king's subjects. Esther couldn't approach the king without him first calling her. If she went before him without being asked, she could die. This is why it was particularly frightening when Mordecai sent word to Esther, telling her of Haman's plan to kill all of the Jewish people and asking her to go to the king and beg for mercy.

Esther thought, "I can't..... I just can't! I could be killed." Esther was fearful, but she was persuaded when she understood that God had placed her there at this time to help bring deliverance to her people.

Esther was used at just the right time to save God's people. Now, we wait for another that will come... at just the right time.

*Is it possible God has placed you where you are? "For such a time as this"? Discuss with one another possible ways you can share God's love with others. Pick one of those ideas and do it during Advent. Pray that God would reveal to you and your family more and more ways to serve Him and others.*

# SILENCE

SU M TU W TH F SA

*"........................."*

*— God*

In my Bible there is a single page that separates the Old and the New Testament.

One. Blank. Page. This page represents 400 years of history.

Four hundred years where, as the story goes, God said nothing.

Four hundred years of silence.

After thousands of years of waiting and seeing promises fulfilled, thousands of years of prophets warning and experiencing God's hand of blessing and correction, after being led through the wilderness by the pillar of fire and led into battle for the Promised Land. The chaos of the time of the Judges. The glory of King David. The temple built by Solomon. The captivity. The exile. The restoration. And now, SILENCE.

Still.
No.
Savior.

When God blesses, we rejoice. When He disciplines, we weep. But when there is silence, what do we do?

When there is silence, loneliness is felt more deeply. When there is silence, we are faced with the echo of our own thoughts. When there is silence, there is confusion.

The people were walking in darkness……

But things are not always as they seem. God was busy at work, setting the stage. He was further preparing the world for what was to come.

> God was uniting the world with a common language.
> God was connecting the remote places with roads.
> He was at work.
> So that, at just the right time…..

His --- Message ---- Would ---- Go --- Forth!

The wait is almost over.

Sometimes the holiday season can be difficult. For some, there is silence where there was once laughter. There is loneliness where there was once companionship. There is confusion in the celebrations and sorrows. But take heart. God is at work! We wait for our comforter.

*Make a phone call, write a note, or plan a visit with someone you know is having a difficult time this holiday season. Do not forget about them in your prayers.*

*If the holidays are difficult for you then please reach out to those around you for comfort and support. Pray for strength during these hard days.*

# SHEPHERDS
DECEMBER 22

SU M TU W TH F SA

*The people who walked in darkness have seen a great light. For those*
*who lived in a land of deep shadows – light! Sunbursts of Light!*
*– Isaiah 9:2 (MSG)*

After many years of darkness, a brilliant light burst forth. After generations of what seemed like silence, as if God had put humankind aside, came a voice in the night. After so much waiting, the time at last was here.

Beneath the blazing, angelic warrior-herald, a group of humble men tended their flocks. Perhaps the angel wondered why he had been sent to cowering shepherds.

Why was he not sent to Herod, in his wondrous palace and regal retinue?[31] Or to the priests in the Temple, the spiritual elite with their rites and rituals? Or to the Pharisees, who strive so hard for righteousness?

Or maybe to that zealous group, the ones whose fanatical devotion led them to leave their normal lives and pursue a hopeless military campaign against oppressive Rome?

No, he had been sent to the lowest of men to proclaim the coming of the Messiah, to proclaim that the beautiful Word of God had become flesh. He was sent to proclaim the gospel, and so he did.

"Fear not, for behold, I bring you good news of great joy that will be for all the people. For unto you is born this day in the city of David a Savior, who is Christ the Lord. And this will be a sign for you: you will find a baby wrapped in swaddling cloths and lying in a manger." (Luke 2:10-12, ESV)

The Shepherds beneath were still considering the bold proposition of "Fear not!" when suddenly the sky was filled. The angelic host of heaven appeared, bathed in light. One angel had driven them to quake with fear; now a whole army of angels proclaimed:

"Glory to God in the highest, and on earth peace among those with whom he is pleased!"

The shepherds were terrified, yet filled with joy!

Then, just as quickly as they had appeared, the angels were gone – returned to their celestial place. The lowly shepherds decided to go see what had been miraculously revealed to them. They left their flocks, risking their livelihoods, and sought out the baby that the angels had told them about.

They had already seen one incredible thing that night; a thing that moved them to trembling, tears, and laughter. Now they were on their way to the little town of Bethlehem, to a dirty little stable, to find a mom and a dad, and a baby lying in a little manger. When they saw this, they would see the little One that would change them and the world forever.

God was very intentional in choosing those men to hear the Gospel first. From the very beginning, the Gospel was for the poor, the broken, and the outcast. From the very beginning, all who would leave their flocks behind them could receive the Good News.

*The shepherds would have missed out had they not left their flocks; what is God asking you to leave behind to see Him better? Pray today for the clarity and strength to leave behind anything that hinders you from seeing Him.*

# MAGI
DECEMBER 23

SU M TU W TH F SA

*"Where is the one who has been born king of the Jews? We saw his*
*star when it rose and have come to worship him."*
*– Matthew 2:2 (NIV)*

What could convince you to leave your home? For what reason would you take a dangerous and difficult journey for days, the burning sun above and harsh desert beneath, with nothing but a few camels?

For a group of wealthy, wise, and influential men, the answer to that question was that they saw something new in the sky. New lights appearing in the sky is something that does not happen. These men had studied the skies their whole lives, but this was the very first *new thing* that they had ever seen or heard of. It was a new, bright shining star in the cold, dark, quiet sky.

These men were intrigued by this new star, so they studied and sought out its meaning. They made the most astonishing discovery; a new King was born to the Jews.

These were wise men; Magi of the East. They were connected and educated. They had heard of the births of kings and emperors before, but they hadn't heard of anything like this. This was new. This was different. This King was special. This King had his own star!

The Magi had to find out more about this star and King, so they went and sought Him out.

The men loaded up their camels and hit the sand. Their long journey took them to Jerusalem. The searchers, being wise, thought the best place to look for a new king was in the palace.

When they arrived at the palace, they didn't find a new king; instead they found "Herod the Great" and his children. Upon meeting Herod, the Magi enquired about the arrival of the new King of the Jews. Herod was shocked and terrified. If anyone should have known or heard about a new king, it was he! After all, Herod was the king of the Jews. But he had heard nothing.

Herod summoned all of his trusted advisers, the priests, and scribes to find out what the Magi were talking about. These scholars, who missed the star in the first place, confirmed where the Messiah was to be born. The Magi were sent to Bethlehem, the city of David.

Herod's jealousy conspired against the Magi and the Messiah. "When you find him," Herod commanded the Magi, doing his best to conceal his true murderous plan, "come tell me right away. I want to worship him, too." However, God sent a vision and warned the Magi not to tell Herod anything.

When the Magi from the East finally arrived in Bethlehem, the star above reappeared and their hearts were filled with an incredible joy. The warm light guided them to Mary, Joseph, and a small child. As the boy lay there in the manger playing, they bowed down and worshipped Him, presenting Him with gifts of gold, frankincense, and myrrh. Strange gifts for a baby, but wonderful and perfect gifts for the King.

The Wise Men sought out and found the King. Was He King of the Jews? Yes. But He was also the King of this group of foreigners from the East. It is on this King that we wait.

*Is He your King? What is stopping you from asking Him to rule your heart and life? Take this opportunity to ask anyone in your family if they want to ask Christ to be the King of their heart [Refer to page 78 for "How Do I Become a Christian"]. Pray for your lost loved ones today*

# MARY AND JOSEPH
DECEMBER 24

SU M TU W TH F SA

*The Lord himself shall give you a sign; Behold a virgin shall conceive,*
*and bear a son, and shall call his name Immanuel.... Blessed art thou*
*among women, and blessed is the fruit of thy womb.*
*– Isaiah 7:14; Luke 1:42 (KJV)*

Mary was young, and she had lived her whole life in the small, insignificant town of Nazareth. She wasn't looking for excitement, and did her best to honor God with her life. Mary looked forward to living a quiet and fruitful life with Joseph, the man to whom she was engaged.

As she was going about her daily routine -- fetching water from the town well, gathering food from the garden, and helping her mom and dad in any way possible -- she heard a voice: "Greetings, Mary!" The voice startled her because last time she checked, no one else was there. As she turned to see who spoke, the voice continued: "You are highly favored because God is with you!"

To Mary's astonishment, the voice belonged to an angel, and not just any angel, but the angel Gabriel. The presence of Gabriel and the words he spoke frightened her. She did not understand. After all, she was just a simple, small town girl. Why would God take notice of her?

"Mary, do not be afraid. God has sent me to tell you that, even though you are a virgin, you will give birth to a son. He will be the Son of the Most High and will sit on the throne of His father, David. He will reign forever. This will happen when the Holy Spirit's power overshadows you. Are you willing to walk this path that Yahweh has laid out for you?"

Mary replied, "I am the Lord's servant. I am willing." Excited by what had just happened, she ran to tell the news to her relative, Elizabeth.

\*\*\*

Joseph was an honorable man. He had worked hard learning the family business and had become a skilled carpenter. He faithfully worked each day, knowing that it was his skills and his calloused hands that would provide for his future family. He loved Mary and looked forward to the family he would share with her. A few long days and some blisters on his hands were a small price to pay to provide a home for the family that God would provide.

One day as he was swinging his hammer, he heard mutters and murmurs in the street. The rumors got louder and clearer and when Joseph figured out what was being said, his heart sank. Mary, the one that was to be his wife, was pregnant. Joseph knew one thing for certain; the baby she was carrying was not his. This news crushed Joseph. He felt betrayed, angry, hurt, lied-to, alone, and confused. But most of all, he was sad.

Joseph sat there in shock, staring at the wall. He loved Mary and, even though he felt hurt by her, he did not want her to endure any more pain than she already would. He didn't want her to face public disgrace. So Joseph, being honorable, decided he would secretly call off the engagement. It would have to wait until morning, though, because it was getting late and now it was time to sleep.

As Joseph slept, an angel came to him in a dream and said, "Joseph, you need to take Mary as your wife. She has not wronged you. The baby that she now carries was conceived through the power of the Holy Spirit. This baby will be a boy and you will give him a special name because he will save people from their sins."

When Joseph awoke, he obeyed the LORD and took Mary to be his wife. Soon the blessed fruit of Mary's womb will come. Soon the wait will be over.

*As we near the end of our wait take some time to marvel at how God worked His plan from the very beginning. Pray together, worshiping God*

# CHRIST
DECEMBER 25

SU M TU W TH F SA

*Now in those days a decree went out from Caesar Augustus to register all the empire for taxes.... Everyone went to his own town to be registered. So Joseph also went up from the town of Nazareth in Galilee to Judea, to the city of David called Bethlehem, because he was of the house and family line of David. He went to be registered with Mary, who was promised in marriage to him, and who was expecting a child. While they were there, the time came for her to deliver her child. And she gave birth to her firstborn son and wrapped him in strips of cloth and laid him in a manger, because there was no place for them in the inn.*
*– Luke 2:1-7 (NET)*

The scene is complete: Mary and Joseph are huddled together, their hearts filled with love as they gaze upon their new baby boy. The shepherds and their sheep sneak into the stable to catch a peek of the baby that the angels told them about. The cows, donkey, and camels are all in their stalls. and perhaps even a hound dog named Charlie is wagging his tail as he sits in the corner. The Magi -- well, the Magi are still on their way. (Ask your pastor about that!)

All eyes are fixed on the baby who is wrapped in rags and resting in the feeding trough. He is the one that will be the light in the darkness. His presence will fill the empty places. He will bring peace to the chaos and He will make us new creations.

We have waited and now He is here!

He is the Door .

He is our Ark of Protection.

He is our Refuge and Strength.

He is the Promise Keeper.

He is the Sacrificial Lamb of God.

He is the one upon whom angels ascend and descend.

He is the one from Nazareth.

He is the Betrayed Savior.

He is Our Freedom.

He gives us the Spirit of Power.

He is Our Victor.

He is Judge and King.

He is the Bread of Life.

He is the kingmaker.

He grew from the branch of Jesse.

He is the descendant of David that comes to renew hearts.

He is the Ready and Willing Prophet.

He will write the Law of Love on our hearts.

He walks with us in the furnace and closes the mouths of lions.

He repairs broken places and He came at just the right time.

He is our Comfort and Peace.

He is the True Shepherd.

He is the Good News.

He is the star that shows the way and lights the hearts of all.

He is so much more and He has a great plan for you!

He is Jesus!

He is Christ, the King of kings!

### MERRY CHRISTMAS!

*Before you open your gifts, take some time to consider the greatest gift given to all people. Have you received this gift? Take some time to thank the Father, Son, and Holy Spirit for all He has done. Find a way to keep Christ the center of your celebrations today*

# HOW DO I BECOME
# A CHRISTIAN?

*For this is the way God loved the world: He gave his one and only Son, so that everyone who believes in him will not perish but have eternal life. – John 3:16(NET)*

Some people think a personal relationship with God is something only pastors and super-religious people can understand. Others think that if they simply live a good enough life, they can earn God's love and have a relationship with Him. God's plan of salvation is simple enough for anyone to understand and it is not something we can earn. So, how can we be made right with God? Here are the **A – B – C's** to enter into a relationship with God.

### Admit

Admit to God that you are a sinner. Everyone needs salvation because we all have a problem that the Bible calls sin. Sin is living, being, and acting how we want to, rather than how God created us. Sin is knowing to do right, but doing wrong anyway. Sin is rebellion against God our Creator. All who do not live a life of perfect obedience to God are guilty of sin. None of us are perfect. The Bible teaches, "All have sinned and fall short of the glory of God." (Rom. 3:23 NET) Since none of us are perfect, that means all of us are sinners. (Rom. 3:10- 18)

The result of sin is spiritual death (Rom. 6:23 NET). Spiritual death means eternal separation from God. Since we are guilty of sin, we are subject to the punishment for sin, which is spiritual death (separation from God). That means the first thing we need to do is admit that we are sinners and separated from God. Is this something you have admitted? Is this something you can admit now? If so, that is the first step in repentance and returning to your Creator.

## Believe

We are not able to erase our sin, but there is One who can. His name is Jesus and He has been the focus of this book and the Advent and Christmas seasons. After you have admitted your sin, you need to believe in Jesus Christ and receive the free gift of forgiveness of your sin. Forgiveness is available to all of us because, even though we have sinned, God loves each of us. Because he loves us, God offers us salvation.

The Bible says that, "God demonstrates his own love for us in that while we were still sinners, Christ died for us." (Rom. 5:8 NET) We didn't do anything to deserve His love and salvation. In fact, just the opposite is true! The penalty for sin is death. That is a price we cannot pay, so Jesus paid it for us on the cross. Now we just need to put our faith in him. The Bible says, "For this is the way God loved the world: He gave his one and only Son, so that everyone who believes in him will not perish but have eternal life." (John 3:16 NET) Do you believe that Christ died for your sins in order for you to be able to have a relationship with God?

## Confess

If you have been able to admit your sin and you believe Jesus died for you, then all that is left is to confess. To confess simply means to declare your faith in Christ. The Bible teaches, "If you confess with your mouth that Jesus is Lord and believe in your heart that God raised him from the dead, you will be saved. For with the heart one believes and thus has righteousness and with the mouth one confesses and thus has salvation." (Rom. 10:9-10 NET)

Take some time and pray. Tell God the faith you have in His son, Jesus. Tell others about it. Contact your pastor, and if you do not have a pastor, contact a local church and talk to the pastor there. Tell your friends and family members. Seek out baptism and become part of a church so that others who have put their trust in Christ can walk with you.

# Love on Trial

## A Walk Through Passion Week With Jesus

Chuck Sanford

Kayte Sanford

# MONDAY

*"'My house shall be called a house of prayer,'"*
Matthew 21:13 (ESV)

It's Monday morning.

The streets of Jerusalem are packed. Thousands of people are pouring into the city streets for Passover. Some of them are from Jerusalem and the surrounding towns; others have been traveling for weeks on foot. Jesus and His disciples are in the crowd of weary people pressing along toward the Temple.

As they approach the outer courts, they see something that hits Jesus in the pit of His stomach. It's hard for us to imagine Jesus getting angry, maybe because He didn't get angry at the same things you and I do. He didn't get angry when people cursed Him, or when His own neighbors tried to kill Him, or when things didn't go His way. When people were rude, when they broke all the rules of polite behavior and societal expectation, Jesus responded with mercy and grace.

But now Jesus is angry because people have turned the Temple into something disgusting. It is supposed to be a place of prayer. It is supposed to be a place where tired and hurting souls could find some help. It is supposed to be a place where the ignorant, those who don't know about God, can be  educated.

It is supposed to be a place where God is glorified; instead, it had become a place where someone tried to sell Him an overpriced pigeon. Instead, it had become a place where the poor were taken advantage of. Instead, it had become a place where the rich get richer and people made money at the expense of their souls.

Jesus sees this injustice, and He is angry. He enters into the inner court, flips the tables and chases out the thieves.

**Take a Closer Look:**

To read about these events check out -  Matthew 21:12-17, Mark 11:12-19, Luke 19:45-48

**Reflection:**

*We want to be like Jesus. That means showing grace and mercy to people who tick us off. It doesn't mean ignoring injustice. Spend some time praying about the injustices in our world.*

*Are there any injustices God is calling you to take action against?*

# TUESDAY

*"The stone that the builders rejected has now become the cornerstone.*
*That is the Lord's doing, and it is marvelous in our eyes."*
*Matthew 21:42 (ESV)*

It is only three days until the cross. This fact weighs heavily on Jesus' mind, but His friends and followers are still oblivious. The disciples don't realize that Our Lord is choosing to spend some of His last time teaching at the Temple.

However, the Pharisees and Sadducees, the religious leaders of the time, have become very agitated by Christ because He challenged their ways and leadership simply by speaking the truth. The religious leaders decided that they need to stop Jesus, and so, they set out to trick Him in order to stop His ministry.

The leaders question Jesus on where His authority comes from and whether He even has a right to speak the things He is saying. They question Jesus about both Jewish and Roman law, as well as religious doctrine. Each question is an attempt to get Jesus to say something that will get Him in trouble, either with Rome or with the people.

Jesus sees the true motive behind each line of questioning, . Yet, He responds with truth, grace, and wisdom -- revealing the heart of God for all people.

Even though the religious leaders were highly favored in their community, and seen as righteous and upstanding men of the law, Jesus saw the truth of their hearts. He knew they were selfish, hateful, and deceiving. He called them "white washed tombs": on the outside they *looked* nice, but all their insides were dead. Christ warned the people about following leaders like this, and warns us of being like them ourselves. It is not about the outward appearances, the religious acts we carry out, the organizations we are involved in. That is all just pride, just a white wash.

We need to be careful that, like the Pharisees and Sadducees, we are not so caught up in the things of this world that we miss JESUS! What truly matters is the love of God, seeking Him, and allowing our hearts to be transformed. It is about love. It is about the HEART!

**Take a Closer Look:**

To read about these events check out  Matthew 21:23-23:39, Mark 11:27-12:44, Luke 20:1-21:4.

**Reflection:**

*Are there areas in your life where  you are more concerned with outward appearances than inward growth?*

*Are there people/things of the world that you are following and listening to that are not in line with the heart of God?*

*Spend time in prayer with Jesus. Draw close to Him today and allow His love to change you from the inside out.*

# WEDNESDAY

*"Then one of the twelve, whose name was Judas Iscariot, went to the chief priests and said, 'What will you give me if I deliver him over to you?'"*
*Matthew 26:14-15 (ESV)*

*Judas.*

If I were to call you Judas, you would know that I meant you were a treacherous, unfaithful backstabber. Judas' sin was so terrible and tragic that for thousands of years even his name has meant "evil."

It is a normal Wednesday. The Chief Priests have sent Judas a message asking to meet; it would be rude to refuse. So the disciple slips away from the group. No one knows what he intends as he walks down that lonely city street, and meets with men who plan to murder his friend.

For three years, Judas had followed Jesus. They had been through so much together. The excitement of miracles and the overwhelming popularity that came as thousands of people were fed and healed and loved; the pain and fear as some of those same people turned on them, like when they were nearly stoned to death in Nazareth.

It's easy to assume that Judas has been evil and unfaithful from the start, but if this were the case, we would expect him to have left before this time. We know he is trusted, he even has a good reputation. He isn't a hothead like John and James, or a boaster like Peter, or a former tax collector, or a zealot. He is the one Jesus chose to be the "purse keeper," a position of trust.

What we cannot know from outward appearances is that Judas harbors sin in his heart. He has been stealing little bits from his friends for some time. Never anything big, never enough to be noticed by the other disciples, but enough to make him spiritually weak. It is because of this spiritual compromise, this hidden sin, that he is vulnerable. When Satan attacks, Judas does exactly what the devil wants.

Judas makes a deal with those who want Jesus dead. The religious leaders, with murder in their hearts, offer him thirty silver pieces, and Judas takes it. Maybe they give him false assurances, or maybe he figures Jesus will simply work a miracle to escape. Maybe he has all the excuses we can think of, but he still does the unthinkable: he trades the perfect Son of God for thirty coins.

**Take a Closer Look:**

To read about these events check out Matthew 26:1-16 , Mark 14:1-11, Luke 22:1-6.

**Reflection:**

*Do you have sin you're trying to hide in your heart?*

*Are you making lame excuses for not doing what God wants?*

*Secret sins can create a foothold for Satan. Spend some time in prayer confessing the sins of your heart and allow God to forgive you and heal the weak and wounded areas in your life.*

# THURSDAY

*"I do not ask for these only, but also for those who will believe in me through their word,"*
John 17:20 (ESV)

It is Jesus' last day before He is to die. He is about to be beaten, tortured, and murdered. He is going to be betrayed by one of his closest friends. His other friends will abandon Him, and even even deny they knew Him. Jesus is in agony. He cries out to God to please let there be another way, please spare Him this tragedy.

Yet even in the midst of the terrifying prospects He is facing, Jesus turns His heart toward others. He chooses God's will over His own. He chooses to show God's heart to those around Him.

Jesus spent His last evening serving His disciples, washing their feet, teaching them, and offering words of comfort for the times ahead. He is about to be tortured and killed, but He is offering comfort to His friends instead.

Not only does Jesus spend His last night showing, by his own example, a servant's heart, but He spends time in prayer as well. He prays that His suffering can be avoided and that there can be another way. He also prays for strength to carry out God's will.

He prays for His disciples, who won't even stay awake and pray with Him.

He prays for you and me!

His last night, as He prepares for the greatest trial anyone has ever faced, Jesus turned His focus to *US!* He chose to serve, heal, and pray for those around Him. He chose to put LOVE first!

**Take a Closer Look:**

To read about these events check out Matthew 26:17-75, Mark 14:12-74, Luke 22:7-65, John 13:21-18:27.

**Reflection:**

*In our biggest trials, how can we follow Jesus' example and choose to be 'others' focused? Do you think this would help make the trials more bearable?*

*Look at Jesus' prayer for us in John 17: 20- 26. Reflect on the words that He prayed for you. How does this impact your life?*

*This is also the day that Jesus established communion as a way to remember Him and His love. Spend some time in prayer, remembering Jesus and thanking Him for who He is and all He has done. Ask forgiveness for the times that, like the disciples, you "fell asleep on the job" or abandoned Him in a time of need.*

# FRIDAY

*"It is Finished."*
*-John 19:30 (ESV)*

Good Friday.

It's an odd name for a day when our Savior suffered so much.

Before the sun has risen, Jesus is dragged before an illegal and corrupt court. People make up lies about Him, and, even though their false stories don't add up, they still convict Him.

Roughly bound by those priests, Jesus is dragged in front of Roman consul, Pilate. Jesus again listens to lies heaped up against him, only to be sent away to Herod. A third time they accuse Him, but Herod sends Him back to Pilate.

He's pushed in front of a crowd of those He came to save. He turns His head to see another prisoner beside Him.

"Who do you want, Jesus or Barabbas?" Pilate shouts.

Those He came for cheer for the murderer Barabbas.

Then they flog *Love* Himself. Thirty-nine lashes with a nine-pronged whip leave His back and sides a mess of gore. I wonder what hurt more: having His body beaten by that cruel whip, or hearing those He came to save, those He loves, cheer for them to do it?

Jesus, the carpenter's son, is given a beam of wood to carry. It is placed across His wounded back and He is led through the crowded Jerusalem streets to the place called "Skull."

Then *Love* Himself falls. Jesus, the carpenter's son, is now too weak to carry a single a beam of wood. That's how badly He is hurt. A man named Simon is pulled out of the crowd and forced to carry the crossbeam. People continue to crowd Him, some screaming for His blood, others crying and weeping. *Love* prays for them as He walks.

When they arrive at that place, they begin the crucifixion. First, each hand has a large nail driven through it, connecting it to the beam. Then they put a third nail through His feet. The cross is lifted into position, jarring his battered body. His head and shoulders slump forward, and the weight of His body hangs on the nails and pushes on His lungs. In order to breathe, He has to pull Himself up on the nails; it's only a slight movement, but it makes speaking excruciating.

*Even now, Love Himself prays for His murderers. He prays for their forgiveness because He loves them even as they kill Him.*

*Even on the cross, Love is forgiving the sins of those who come to Him.*

*Even on the cross, Love is comforting us.*

*Even on that brutal plank of wood, Jesus is fully human, thirsting and broken, but loving you and me.*

*Even then, He is declaring "It is Finished." Your life of sin, your bondage, your affliction, your debt, all that keeps you separated from God, is finished.*

Knowing what His death accomplished, He gave up His Spirit and died.

**Take a Closer Look:**

To find out more check out Psalm 22, John 19, Mark 15, Luke 22:66-23:56, Matthew 27.

**Reflection:**

*Spend some time with our Lord in prayer today. Reflect on the sacrifice He made for you!*

# SATURDAY

*"[They told Pilate], "Sir, we remember how the imposter said, while he
was still alive,'After three days I will rise.'..."*
*Matthew 27:63 (NLT)*

Jesus is dead. *Love* Himself is dead.

His followers mourn their loss from afar, as they cannot go see him on the Sabbath. Their hopes of restoration are dashed, their leader is gone…they are defeated. Or so they think.

Meanwhile, the Pharisees who claim to be confident that Jesus was no more than a deceiver, fear Him, even in death. They are afraid of Jesus' promise that He would rise again. They are afraid of the movement Jesus has started among His followers and what they might do. They are so afraid of this CORPSE that they have His tomb sealed and soldiers stationed outside to guard the body. They are afraid…and for good reason.

**Take a Closer Look:**

To read about these events check out Matthew 27:62-66, Mark 16:1.

**Reflection:**

*Imagine being in the shoes of the disciples and thinking that Jesus really was gone. Where would you be without Him? How far has He brought you in your life?*

*Even the Pharisees, who did not believe in Jesus, were afraid of the power He held. Do you truly believe and acknowledge the fullness of His power? Take a minute to reflect on who He is and what He is capable of.*

*Spend some time in prayer today thanking Jesus for what He has done in your life and the life-changing power that He brings into all of our lives.*

# SUNDAY!

*"He isn't here! He is risen from the dead!"*
Luke 24:6 (NLT)

*The tragedy is over and Jesus is alive!*
*Victory has come and our sins have been forgiven!*

We, as sinners, were separated from God, unable to be in relationship with Him. We were dead in our sins, doomed to spend eternity without God. But because Jesus went to the cross and died, he took the penalty for our sins.

Now, because Jesus rose again, the power of death is destroyed forever!

Jesus rose again, and in Him we can have new life!

Jesus rose from the dead and now, through the Holy Spirit, we can have a relationship with God -- no longer separated from God by our sin!

Jesus is alive and we can live everyday in fellowship with Him. We can be loved, healed, and made whole…all because of JESUS!

If you do not have a relationship with Jesus, and would like to, you can pray the following:

*"God, I know that I have broken your laws and my sins have separated me from you. I am truly sorry, and now I want to turn away from my past sinful life toward you. Please forgive me, and help me avoid sinning again. I believe that your son, Jesus Christ died for my sins, was resurrected from the dead, is alive,*

*and hears my prayer. I invite Jesus to become the Lord of my life, to rule and reign in my heart from this day forward. Please send your Holy Spirit to help me obey You, and to do Your will for the rest of my life. In Jesus' name I pray, Amen."*

You are forgiven. You are loved. You are treasured. And Jesus is Alive!

## TODAY WE CELEBRATE!!!

**Take a Closer Look:**

To read more check out Matthew 28:1-7, Mark 16:2-8, Luke 24:1-12, John 20: 1-18.

**Reflection:**

*Take time today to celebrate and give thanks for all that Christ accomplished on the cross and through His resurrection.*

*If you have made a decision to follow Christ today, or would like to find out more about this, please talk to your local pastor or a trusted Christian friend.*

# END NOTES

1. Bratcher, Dennis. "The Meaning of Church Colors". *CRIVOICE.org*. 2012.
2. Just go to Pinterest.com and type "Jesse Tree" in the search box.
3. Psalm 121:1-2
4. A benediction, simply put, is a prayer of blessing.
5. Genesis 3:15
6. 1 Peter 3:18-22
7. Genesis 1:28, 9:1, 9:7
8. Hamilton, Victor. "Handbook on the Pentateuch." page 82
9. Hebrews 6:13
10. Hebrews 11:17-19
11. He named the place "Bethel." but before he named it he proclaimed that it was the Gate of Heaven, See Genesis 28:16-19
12. See Genesis 32
13. John 1:51, 14:6
14. Deuteronomy 25:5-10
15. Genesis 38:9
16. John 1:46
17. Joseph's story takes up much of the book of Genesis. To get all the exciting details see Genesis 37-50
18. Exodus 3:13-15
19. Numbers 32:13
20. Deuteronomy 6:4-9
21. Leviticus 19:9-10, 23:22; Deuteronomy 24:19-21
22. 1 Samuel 9:9
23. Casting lots was a method used to determine the will of God. It was a game of chance thought understood to be controlled by God "The lot is cast into the lap, but its every decision is from the LORD," (Prov. 16:33 NIV).
24. 1 Samuel 17:12-15
25. 1 Samuel 3:14; Acts 13:22
26. 2 Samuel 7:8-17
27. Malachi 4:5-6
28. Jeremiah 8:11
29. Jeremiah 23:1-8, 33:14-16
30. Daniel 1:4-5
31. Retinue is a group of advisors, assistants, or others accompanying an important person (i.e. an entourage).

# ABOUT THE AUTHORS

TJ Torgerson is the pastor of Goodhope Church of the Nazarene in Missouri. He graduated with honors from Nazarene Bible College, where he earned a BA in Bible & Theology. He and his wife Nacomi have been married for 15 years. They have 4 sons; Josiah, Caleb, Zack, and Joe. The first born, Josiah, went to be home with the Lord.

Chuck Sanford is the pastor of Prescott Valley Church of the Nazarene. He graduated from Nazarene Bible College with a BA in Bible & Theology. His wife, Kayte, serves God full-time in the field of special education. Their ministry is to share the gospel with everyone, and they have the skills to make sure that "everyone" includes those with special needs. They also have a special calling towards foster and adoption, and have one son, Isaac.

# THANK YOU.

Thank you for purchasing this devotional book. All proceeds from the sale of *Awaiting Christmas: A Family Devotional for Advent* go to support the work and ministry of Goodhope Church of the Nazarene. We pray this book will be a blessing to you and your family and beneficial for your spiritual formation.

Made in United States
North Haven, CT
23 November 2021

11444677R00063